How the
Polish
Created
CANADA

JACEK KOZAK

DRAGON
HILL

© 2011 by Dragon Hill Publishing Ltd.
First printed in 2011 10 9 8 7 6 5 4 3 2 1
Printed in Canada

The Publisher: Dragon Hill Publishing Ltd.

Library and Archives Canada Cataloguing in Publication

Kozak, Jacek

How the Polish created Canada / Jacek Kozak.

Includes bibliographical references.

ISBN 978-1-896124-56-8

1. Polish people—Canada—History. 2. Polish Canadians—History. I. Title.

FC106.P7K685 2011   971.00491'85   C2011-905911-8

Project Director: Gary Whyte
Project Editor: Kathy van Denderen
Production: Tamara Eder
Cover Image: Textured background, Red background, Scrollwork, Polish Eagle, Cherry Blossoms, Maple Leaves: © Photos.com

Photo Credits: Every effort has been made to accurately credit the sources of photographs. Any errors or omissions should be reported directly to the publisher for correction in future editions. Photographs courtesy of Archives of Ontario (p. 18, W.J. Topley; p. 29), Canada Science and Technology Museum (p. 103, CN000987), Glenbow Museum (p. 45, NA-3091-36; p. 47, NA-3091-91; p. 59, NA-3091-96), Holy Rosary Archives (p. 53), Library and Archives Canada (pp. 15, 21), Wikipedia (pp. 36, 39, Gpski), www.dworekwymyslowo.pl (p. 233), Zurakowski Park (pp. 88, 90, 93).

Produced with the assistance of the Government of Alberta, Alberta Multimedia Development Fund

Government of Alberta ■

We acknowledge the support of the Canada Council for the Arts which last year invested $20.1 million in writing and publishing throughout Canada.

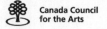

Canada Council   Conseil des Arts
for the Arts   du Canada

PC: 1

CONTENTS

INTRODUCTION. 5

CHAPTER 1: RIGHT FROM THE START 9

CHAPTER 2: LITTLE POLAND IN CANADA . . . 32

CHAPTER 3: IN SEARCH OF LAND 43

CHAPTER 4: PLEASE HELP WITH THE WAR . . 65

CHAPTER 5: ŻURA AND FRIENDS. 83

CHAPTER 6: THE POLES ARE COMING 97

CHAPTER 7: POLES STANDING TALL. 116

CHAPTER 8: MORE THAN JUST PEROGIES . . 146

CHAPTER 9: ALL OVER THE COUNTRY. 170

CHAPTER 10: THREE PERSONAL STORIES OF
POLISH CANADIANS. 182

APPENDIX 1: POLISH ORGANIZATIONS IN
CANADA 201

APPENDIX 2: IT PAYS TO BE CANADIAN 232

NOTES ON SOURCES 237

DEDICATION

For Magda, who made it all possible, and Adam,
the true Polish Canadian

ACKNOWLEDGEMENTS

I extend words of gratitude to all the authors referred
to in the text—without your painstaking research, this
vast subject could never have been covered adequately.

In particular, I would like to thank Dr. Anna
Reczyńska of the Jagiellonian University in Kraków in
Poland, the foremost Polish expert on Polish immigration to Canada. I gratefully acknowledge ready assistance of the Canadian Polish Research Institute in
Toronto for their help in obtaining access to often forgotten and out-of-print publications.

The people mentioned above contributed greatly to
this book; any errors or omissions are exclusively mine.

INTRODUCTION

POLISH FOOTPRINTS

A small atoll in the middle of the Pacific Ocean called Christmas Island, or Kiritimati, has the greatest land area of any coral atoll in the world, according to Wikipedia. It is the home of only about 5000 inhabitants, mainly Micronesians, living in four villages. The fifth village, formerly called Paris, has been abandoned. The names of the other four are telling: the biggest one bears the proud name of London, while one of the remaining three is listed as "Poland." How? Why? Who gave such an exotic name to a palm-studded village on the antipodes? No one really knows. One thing is certain, some enterprising Pole must have visited the island and named the village after his native country.

The story of Poland, Kiritimati, has been cited as proof that there is probably no place in the world, with all its most remote corners, where traces of Polish presence could not be found. The same applies to Canada. Polish Canadians rarely appear in Canadian history textbooks and are hardly ever listed among the ethnic groups who built and shaped modern Canada. However, a small bay in the Canadian arctic bears the name of Strzelecki Harbour. Paweł Strzelecki was a 19th-century Polish explorer and geologist, but he achieved fame for his work in Australia, not Canada. As far as I could determine, he never made a visit to Canada during his life, so what is his name doing on an uninhabited Nunavut island?

Searching for Polish footprints in the most unusual places seems to be a Polish national pastime. It is as if the Poles needed outside confirmation of their ability, forcefulness and enterprising spirit. We have never been a nation of explorers and conquerors of the world. The one attempt at establishing a Polish colony in Africa in the colonization era of European development ended on a farcical note. Some may interpret this search as looking for a cure to a national inferiority complex; I would rather say that it is a plea for due recognition.

On balance, the Poles did get to unexpected places, survived in the most unpleasant circumstances, endured and showed their merit. And they often contributed meaningfully to the well-being of the communities they joined. After all, Canadians have a Polish entrepreneur to thank for the beautiful parkland around Ontario's pride—Niagara Falls—and a Polish engineer for the stability of Toronto's CN Tower.

Striving for due credit is particularly valid in North America. Chicago is the second largest Polish city in the world, by population, but as a rule, the Poles in America were the butt of most insensitive "Polish jokes" rather than perceived as a nation of builders of the continent. Ironically, one of the four statues decorating the square in front of the White House in Washington commemorates the contribution of a Polish general to the success of the American Revolution. Polish language, linguistically removed further from English than French or German, separated the Poles from their American compatriots. One may venture a theory that Polish fortunes in America are an illustration of the importance of linguistic communication within ethnically diverse societies. Misunderstood and misunderstanding their neighbours, the Poles in America suffered for decades the brand of Polish jokes, waiting for someone to bring forward their achievements. Although, with the onset of political correctness, Polish jokes lost much of their venom and vigour, Polish Americans have yet to receive their right and proper credit in American society.

Canadians never really warmed to Polish jokes, but it does not follow that they recognize the contribution of Polish Canadians to our common success as a nation.

Polish people cannot boast of having discovered Canada, organized it or built the country. They were not there among the trailblazers, discoverers and organizers. More often, they supplied raw strength, endurance and determination in the process of building something designed by someone else. All too frequently, they had to prove they could do the work before the decision-making body allowed them to undertake it. As well as conquering the elements, they had to convince others they were up to the job, or even better.

One of the best-known Polish Canadians, a true world-class expert in his field, test pilot Janusz Żurakowski gained recognition first in the United Kingdom during and after World War II before he could dream of testing out the legendary Avro Arrow. His membership card from the Polish Test Pilots Association bore serial number "2," which meant he was the second person to receive his licence. He spent a few years working in the test pilot academy in Boscombe Down, but it a lot of convincing before Canadian authorities let him fly the Arrow. And he was one of the lucky ones. Many of Żurakowski's Polish colleagues from the Battle of Britain squadrons were accepted into Canada at the end of the war, mainly as farm labourers, in spite of their (in most cases) university education and wartime experience.

This book is not a history of Polish Canadians. Such a volume would be—in Canada—of academic interest only and would have to tell too many individual stories. There is a Polish nook in northeast Ontario, Little Poland in Toronto and some Polish-sounding place names in the Prairies. Poles in Canada may not have established a clearly visible presence and may have not achieved the status of one of the nationalities that *built* Canada. We have, however, helped build the country, and often this help was crucial and noteworthy.

RIGHT FROM THE START

MERCHANT SON

Poland has never been a colonial power. The Poles did not, as a nation, participate in the process of discovering and conquering North America. The first Polish Canadian has, however, been found in the annals of New France from the 17th century, at the beginning of Canada's history. His gravestone in Montmagny, Québec, has vanished through the centuries, but Andre "the Pole" Loup preceded many Irish, Chinese, Italian and Scottish Canadians.

The honour of discovering the first Polish footprints in the northern part of North America is due to a Polish Canadian historian from the University of Ottawa, Jan Grabowski. Andre Loup, or to give him his true name, Andrzej Wilk, came to Québec probably with marquis de Denonville. Loup's name first appears in Canadian documents in 1687. Canadian historians have a problem with his nationality, as in those days, passports and identity cards were not in everyday use. Andre Loup is often listed as German, even though he used a sobriquet "le Polonais," and his wife and daughter were to be known as "les Polonaises."

A brief excursion, however, into the field of history of Poland makes things clear: "loup" in French is a translation of "wolf" in German and "wilk" in Polish. "Wilk" was and is a fairly common name in Poland, and Polish archives list a Polish merchant family by the name Wilk in 17th-century Gdańsk. This trade gateway of Poland to the world was a member of a German-dominated Hanseatic League, so it is quite conceivable that a merchant family sent one of its sons out into the world, and fortune took him to New France. Was he Polish or German? Andre Loup declares himself Roman Catholic, while the majority of German merchant class in Gdańsk were Protestant. I believe the question of Loup's nationality has been settled.

In 1687 Andre Loup married Marie Stiems, and their first child was born in 1689, only to die two weeks later. The couple adopted a three-year old girl, Marie Magdalene, who grew up in their home and later married Blaise Lepage in 1718.

Loup's career on arrival in New France began with the position of marquis de Denonville's servant. He must have made a good impression on his employer, as the governor general of the colony was one of the guests at Andre's and Marie's wedding. The marriage was also an occasion to change his professional career—he quit his job with the governor general and went into partnership with his father-in-law as a stonemason. When marquis de Denonville was recalled to France, Andre Loup stayed in his new country.

In 1694 he took part in the expedition of Pierre Le Moyne d'Iberville against the British forts on Hudson Bay, which did not bring him fortune and fame, but in a way influenced his professional career. From that time, Andre "Le Polonais" Loup, former servant and stonemason, declared himself to be "a navigator." In 1703 he purchased an 11-ton sailing barque and engaged in lumber transport. The limited number of documents that were preserved indicate his growing prestige and fortune in the community. Instead of seeking employment with others, Andre Loup began to employ workers.

The year 1705 was not a good one for the Pole. He quarrelled with a local gunsmith, Jacques Soullard, and won the confrontation but lost in court. This court record is one of the few times his name is mentioned in historical documents, but he was doing fairly well in the local community of merchants, seamen and ship owners. In 1714 he could afford to borrow almost 5000 livres for the construction of a new sailing vessel. Apparently, he was trustworthy enough to have such an enormous sum lent to him and his enterprise merited such an outlay of capital.

Unfortunately, there is little to add to his story. The St. Lawrence River, which for years gave him his income, was also his grave. The certificate of his death, dated June 30, 1719, lists drowning as the cause of death. The circumstances of this incident remain unknown. All we know is that he was buried in

Montmagny on the south shore of St. Lawrence River in today's Québec.

With Andre Loup's death, the Polish contribution to the development of Canada stops for decades. The next chapter was written by a few Poles in the immigration wave of Loyalists after the American War of Independence and unfortunate prisoners of war from the Napoleonic era.

LEGIONNAIRES IN MANITOBA

French emperor Napoleon Bonaparte was a master of propaganda. Promising much to all who would listen, he managed to convince many Poles that it was in his and France's interest to re-establish a free and independent Poland, which barely a few years earlier was wiped off the map by three powers: Russia, Prussia and Austria. Thus, many young Polish patriots joined special regiments, called "Legions," to fight with Napoleon for the Polish national dream. For a while it seemed almost possible, and Napoleon appreciated the courage of his Polish Legionnaires, remarking after one inconclusive battle that had he only Polish troops, he would have won the confrontation. That did not, however, influence his political decisions, and soon the Polish dream of regained independence was brought to a halt when the French emperor's career came to an end. Before the intentions of Napoleon became self-evident, he managed to send one Polish legion to subdue a slave revolt in Haiti, then called San Domingo.

The journey to the Caribbean was a death warrant for almost all the soldiers of the regiment. Most died of malaria and other tropical diseases. Some joined the rebelling slaves, who, after all, were fighting for the same freedom the Poles wanted for their country. That is why one may encounter, unexpectedly, Polish-sounding names in today's Haiti, proudly born by black families descended in part from those brave legionnaires. A handful of the participants of this colonial war lived to fall into the hands of the British, blockading Haiti and sinking French transports to and from the island. On one of these ships, the British found some Polish veterans.

Dispirited and disappointed with Napoleon, and facing the possibility of a long prison term, many Polish officers and soldiers joined a mercenary Swiss regiment—named De Meuron after its commander. On the American continent, the regiment fought in the War of 1812 and the freedom-loving Poles, disappointed with French promises, found themselves serving as hired guns under a Swiss name.

I call them "De Meuron settlers," although the 10 known Polish members of the Red River colony were really from the De Watteville Regiment. Canadian history texts insist, however, on associating all the members of Lord Selkirk's escort with the name De Meuron, even though they came from three different regiments, the third one being British Glengarry Fencibles, which had nothing to do with the Swiss mercenaries.

When the War of 1812 ended, De Meuron and De Watteville remained in Canada on garrison duty and were partially placed under the command of Thomas Douglas, Lord Selkirk for his Red River Settlement experiment. As we know from the history of Canada, the settlement was not a success. Lord Selkirk's settlers lasted no more than 20 years before the colony was wiped from the face of the earth by the conflict with the Métis and the Northwest Company, by winter blizzards, which in 1825 killed 33 settlers, and by floods. In 1826, half the colony left for the United States, and most of the Swiss veterans of the regiments joined that exodus. A few, however, remained. Chronicles list some of their names: Michael Bardowicz, Pierre Gandrowski, Andrew Jankowski, Michael Kaminski, Wojciech Lasota, Laurent Kwilecki, John Wasilowski, Michael Izaak, Antone Sobacki. Legion and De Watteville regiment veteran Andrzej Jankowski is noted in 1833 Red River census books as the owner of one cow with a calf, one ox, two pigs, one canoe, and the father of a 15-year-old daughter. Five years later, he had four daughters and owned a horse, five oxen, five cows with calves, a barn, two stables and a Red River cart.

Freedom for Poland came 100 years later, but for Jankowski and some of his companions, it came to fruition in Manitoba's wilderness.

Twisted Paths

One name immediately springs to mind whenever the subject of Poles in Canada is brought up—Sir Casimir Gzowski. He has been the symbol of the contribution the Poles have made to the development of Canada and Canadian society. His name is associated with Niagara parks and numerous railways in today's Ontario and Québec; 100 years after his death, his family name symbolized the best in Canadian media. Polish Canadians remember him and respect his memory. And yet, there is a strange ambivalence to the life of this symbolic Polish Canadian. It is as if there was something missing or that something was wrong with being described as the Pole who made the most evident contribution to the development of Canada in its early years.

Born in 1813 to a family of minor nobility in Eastern Poland, Casimir Gzowski followed in his father's footsteps as an officer in the Russian Imperial armed forces. Educated in the famous school in Krzemieniec, he began his military career barely in time to prove his patriotism in the struggle for freedom for his country. The November Uprising of 1830 is the most pronounced symbol of Polish Romanticism in the political arena. Started by a conspiracy of young officers, the uprising failed quickly because of lack of popular support.

Sir Casimir Gzowski (1813–98), engineer, businessman and probably the best-known Polish Canadian

After participating in a heroic defence of the Polish capital, Warsaw, Gzowski ended up in an Austrian prison, and two years later the Austrians exported him to the United States. There, Gzowski quickly demonstrated his skills, learning English and obtaining a degree in law, while supporting himself through teaching French, German and fencing. In October 1839 he achieved sufficient rank in Erie society to marry a doctor's daughter, Mary Beebe.

Gzowski's work was not limited to law; he used his military and engineering education and experience surveying land for canals and railway construction. Soon, his work took him to Canada, where in Kingston he met Governor Sir Charles Bagot, a former British ambassador to the court in St. Petersburg, where Sir Charles had made an acquaintance of Casimir Gzowski's father. Impressed with the young Polish nobleman's achievements, Bagot is said to have remarked, "We must keep you in Canada." And they did.

The Canadian chapter in Gzowski's life began in 1842 and ended 56 years later in Toronto. Traces of his work can be found from the Niagara region all the way to Sherbrooke, Québec. He built railways, bridges and roads. He improved Yonge Street and was involved in the Grand Trunk Railway project. His contribution to the undertakings with his Canadian partners was essential; one of the leading capitalists of that time, Luther Hamilton Holton wrote of Gzowski that his "energy, his tact, his thorough knowledge of every detail of his business, combined with a nice sense of humour, render him in my judgment the most desirable associate."

The list of Gzowski's successes is long and impressive. The one defeat of Gzowski and Company came at the hands of the local council of the municipality of Toronto. The jury is still out on whether he lost because of lack of merit or because he was still regarded as a stranger. Whatever the reason, the administration of Toronto had decided not to award the contract to Gzowski and his associates. The railway esplanade on the waterfront of Toronto never got built. Over 30 years later, the same council retained Gzowski to report as a consulting engineer on the plan of coping with the failure of the project and the resulting confusion of railway lines in the city.

Some unpleasantness in the relationship between Gzowski and Toronto authorities remained. Almost half a century later, the council ordered the total destruction of The Hall, one of the most beautiful residences in the city constructed for Sir Casimir Gzowski and his family by a renowned Toronto architect Frederic Cumberland on the site occupied today by Alexandra Park on Bathurst Street.

The Hall was an impressive building and was a focal point of Toronto society life in the mid-1800s. The two-storey brick house on a six-acre lot was complete with conservatories, a garden, a vinery, stables and a lodge for servants. The residence housed the large Gzowski family (Casimir, Mary and their six children) as well as a dog and a gardener with an eight-person family and two hogs. There even was a place for an old cannon, to remind visitors of the military career of the host. The interior was opulently decorated with bric-a-brac, tapestries and an incalculable number of pictures hanging on all walls. Visitors admired the airy

Sir Casimir Gzowski and Lady Gzowski entertaining prominent members of Toronto society

atmosphere of the high-ceilinged rooms, as if forgetting that it was a practical solution—the owner of the residence stood over six feet, two inches.

Casimir Gzowski went from being an exile, an immigrant and romantic hero of the struggle for Polish national freedom, to a wealthy and successful pillar of society. By 1870, he reached retirement age and could deservedly look back on his life and his success. However, there came a challenge he could not resist—the need to build a bridge over Niagara River that joined Fort Erie and Buffalo.

The task was formidable: the river at this point was deep, the current was strong and water levels and ice conditions were highly unpredictable. In sum, it was a difficult project to undertake. But on October 27, 1873, the bridge was officially opened, and the general manager of Grand Trunk, Charles Brydges declared, "There is no other man in this country who could have carried on the work of this bridge or gone through the daily and hourly anxiety which it entailed during the past four years save Colonel Gzowski."

Having shed his professional responsibilities, Gzowski (who was by then 60 years of age and had amassed a sufficient fortune to live off the capital) could devote himself to social duties. He was instrumental in organizing the Dominion Rifle Association whose members annually competed in marksmanship for the Gzowski Cup. He also acted as an organizer and was elected president of the Canadian Society of Civil Engineers, and the highest decoration awarded by the society became known as the Gzowski Medal.

As a president of the Toronto Turf Club, in 1859 Gzowski was a prime factor in the creation of the Queen's Plate, the first organized thoroughbred horse race in North America. He was honoured as an honorary aide-de-camp to Queen Victoria and was also an avid patron of the arts and music, for many years serving as a president of the Toronto Philharmonic Society. He was an organizer of Wycliffe College and a member of the senate of the University of Toronto. His home in The Hall was the location of numerous parties and celebrations attended by the cream of the Toronto society.

Gzowski stayed away from politics, initially refusing Prime Minister John A. Macdonald's request to compete for the Toronto West riding. But Gzowski agreed, although reluctantly, when Macdonald talked him into joining a royal commission on canals in Canada, and he helped Macdonald in financial matters as well as in the prime minister's fight against his political opponents in the 1878 election campaign (or, as Gzowski called them, "the Philistines.") He even acted briefly as an administrator of Ontario when the province was without a lieutenant-governor in 1896–97. His service to Canada and its ruling elite was finally recognized in 1890, when, at 77, he was once again declared a member of titled nobility: Sir Casimir Gzowski, KCMG.

In August 1898, the *Toronto Globe* published his obituary:

> By his death Toronto loses one who for nearly sixty years had occupied a foremost place in the social and industrial life of the community. A man of commanding appearance and dignified bearing, his figure was a familiar one to the people of this city, and one which never passed unnoticed. To those who knew him socially the rare amiability of his character, the charm of his manner, his broad culture and generous hospitality endeared him in an unusual degree.

After his death, Gzowski's widow sold The Hall to the City of Toronto. The council, as if in petty revenge for past conflicts, quickly razed the beautiful building to the ground. No traces of it remain to this day. And if you want to celebrate the achievements of its owner, you have to travel to Niagara Falls and walk the scenic paths of the park by the waterfall.

On March 5, 1963, Canada Post decided to show appreciation for Gzowski's achievements by issuing a postage stamp commemorating his 150th birthday.

Canadian postage stamp honouring Sir Casimir Gzowski

An exemplary success story of an immigrant to Canada? Why, then, do some Polish Canadians demonstrate mixed feelings when his name is brought up? It has been said that near the end of his life, Sir Casimir Gzowski attended a concert by a celebrated Polish pianist, future prime minister of free and independent Poland, Jan Ignacy Paderewski. When the concert ended, Paderewski approached the noble old man and spoke to him in Polish. Gzowski wept. The once-fighter for the independence of Poland had forgotten how to speak Polish.

Sir Casimir Gzowski's life was a textbook example of assimilation of an immigrant into a new country and its culture. He lived long before the politics of multiculturalism were designed and accepted. His success came at a high price—exile from his native national identity. Patriotic Poles feel uncomfortable when thinking of Gzowski's fate.

A century after Casimir Gzowski's death, I had the pleasure of meeting his great-grandson, Peter Gzowski. Peter's career with CBC Radio was a symbol of the best in Canadian journalism and an embodiment of Canadian patriotism in contrast to foreign (read: American) content of Canadian media.

His radio show *Morningside* broadcast on CBC was incredibly popular. What is more, it was also generally praised in the journalistic community. It brought Peter Gzowski renown and respect, and not only in Canada. Through his work he exerted a definite personal influence on the political and cultural consciousness of his audience. *Morningside* became an authority on Canada—often quoted, referred to and cited. Gzowski contributed greatly to shaping the national identity of Canadians and had a definite say in making it unique.

He started his career in 1971 with a CBC Radio show called *This Country in the Morning*. For three years his daily three-hour show presented its listeners with a wide panorama of Canadian affairs related in a lively, attractive manner. The scope of the show was varied: some fragments were simply interesting, while others were of great importance to the nation. Gzowski stressed that all material in his show was to be given an informative background. He believed that often it is not enough to mention an event; in most cases, if it is worth mentioning, it should be presented in a proper context illuminating its importance.

His show presented interviews with politicians and acknowledged important cultural events, but it also became a forum for meeting ordinary people talking about their daily lives. No wonder the program generated an incomparable response from its listeners. The CBC was literally flooded with letters. The show has been described as a mirror, in which present-day Canada can see its face. I have heard it said by a professional colleague of Gzowski that the show is a more authoritative source of information on Canada and Canadian affairs than all the painstakingly researched volumes authored by world-renowned experts. All the more so, as Gzowski was one of the pioneers of presenting Canada's history and traditions in a convincing manner, rebelling against the common misconception that Canada is a country without history. "If you really want to learn something about Canada, past and present, listen to Gzowski's show" was the advice given to me by an eminent Canadian journalist shortly after my arrival in Toronto.

In 1982, after a few years at CBC Television, Gzowski returned to his radio show, renamed by this time as *Morningside*, and continued working on it for the next 15 years. *Morningside* was a daily radio show of legendary importance. It has been calculated that it attracted over one million listeners daily. The show generated material for six highly informative books called The *Morningside Papers*. In Peter Gzowski's 2002 obituary, the *New York Times* described him as "the voice of Canada."

Peter Gzowski did not speak Polish, but his beautiful home in Rockwood housed an impressive library, and one part of it was devoted to books on Poland. "For Canadians, I am too Polish," he told me. "For Poles, too Canadian."

It Pays to be Polish

It seems particularly ironic that one of the very few Poles mentioned in most Canadian history books was not Polish at all. Nils Gustav von Schoultz has been appropriated by Polish popular history writers and given the rank of a Polish officer who led a military unit from the United States to Canada in 1838. He is described as the commanding officer at the battle of Windmill Point and, having lost the battle and taken prisoner, was executed by Canadians for treason. It has been stated many times that the cruel administration of Upper Canada, mindful of its own interest only, hanged a Polish soldier fighting for freedom. The statement has recently been shown to be absolutely false. Thus, von Schoultz deserves an explanation of who he really was and why he has been included in the ranks of Polish freedom fighters of the 19th century.

The man who attempted to free Upper Canada from British rule was born in 1807 in Kuopio, Finland, to Nils Frederik von Schoultz, a local judge, and Johanna Henrika Gripenberg. When Finland was occupied by the Russians, Nils' family escaped to Sweden. Nils Gustav von Schoultz was, therefore, a Finn by birth and a citizen of Sweden. He was brought up and educated in Stockholm, where he graduated from a military academy and received his commission. His military career did not last long; in 1830 he gave up his commission, probably as a result of a scandal connected to unpaid gambling debts.

One year later, von Schoultz heard of a Polish uprising against the Russians. He joined other Swedes and Finns and went to Warsaw to help Polish freedom fighters in their struggle against the tsarist oppression, and he even took part in the notable battle in defence of the Polish capital city. The uprising, however, did not succeed, and von Schoultz ended up in a Russian prison, from where he escaped to France. Altogether, he spent about six months in Poland. That was the extent of his connection with Poland and the Poles.

In France, he continued his military career in the French Foreign Legion, occasionally visiting Florence, Italy, where his sister was pursuing music studies. There he met and married Ann Campbell, a daughter of a rich Scottish merchant. Soon his family expanded by two daughters, and they moved to Stockholm. His father-in-law entrusted him with some business deals, but Nils von Schoultz was not born to be a merchant. In June 1836 he travelled to London on business. From there, without a word to his family, he departed for America.

For unknown reasons, in the United States, von Schoultz did not introduce himself as a Swedish subject but instead claimed to be a Polish officer and a veteran of the 1831 uprising who was forced into exile by the Russian tsarist regime. To add credibility to his claim, he complemented his family name with the Polish-sounding addition of Scholtewskij or Schobtewiski. He also felt that 29 years of age was not old enough for him and he claimed to be 10 years older. In spite of these modifications to his biography, von Schoultz could not acquire a commission in the United States Army, but his attempts at business transactions brought him to Salina, New York, close to the Canadian border.

There he met refugees from Canada, who escaped their land after the 1837 rebellion. The young Swedish firebrand, spoiling for a fight after the unfortunate result of his first try at freedom fighting in Poland, decided it was time to free the lands occupied by the British Crown in Upper Canada. Thus, he came in contact with Patriot Hunters, an organization dedicated to the eviction of the British Empire from North America and the "liberation" of Canada. Von Schoultz joined the Salina lodge and was persuaded by a senior member of the lodge, John Ward Birge, to take part in a raid on British military installations at Wellington in the border town of Prescott.

An attempt to liberate Upper Canada attracted about 300 volunteers, and the organizers managed to obtain sizeable funds, allowing them to find transportation over the St. Lawrence and even to purchase a field cannon. On November 11, 1838, the invasion of Upper Canada by the forces of self-declared general major John Ward Birge began, with a young "Polish" officer anxious to try to topple his second despotic regime.

The whole operation was doomed from the start. The Patriot Hunters lodge was infiltrated by the British intelligence, the invading forces could not even disembark as planned because someone on the shore had raised the alarm and the invaders had to sail away in search of another landing site. In the end, one of the ships in the invading flotilla struck a sandbar, and it was left to the smaller vessel, with von Schoultz on board, to establish a beachhead at Windmill Point.

By this time, Birge decided he had had enough of this adventure; he suddenly felt some undefined stomach pains and returned to the safety of the American shore. American officials learned of the invasion attempt and sent a regular navy vessel to Ogdensburg in New York, where the organizers of the invasion established the headquarters of the operation. The presence of American officials practically concluded the incident. All communications between the forces at Ogdensburg and the 100 volunteers left at Windmill Point were severed.

From a strictly military point of view, the American invaders' chance of success was slim. One of the few strong cards held by the force was the authentic military experience of its accidental commander, Lieutenant von Schoultz. Another one was the geographical layout of the landing area. There was a hill at Windmill Point, a stone building of the mill itself and a configuration of terrain amiable to establishing a defensive position. Windmill Point could have been a good choice for an invasion beachhead, had there really been an invasion of sizeable forces in Upper Canada. As it was, von Schoultz found himself in an unenviable and untenable position because he let himself be governed by youthful fantasy and placed his trust in bitter political outsiders fantasizing about popular support they never had.

On the other hand, the War of 1812 was still relatively fresh in the memory of the administration of Upper Canada. They were not about to dismiss a military action, even though it was amateurish in preparation and mistimed politically. The leaders of Upper Canada assumed the presence of a strong military unit on their territory, armed with field artillery. Whatever the problems of the invasion force, its activity on Canadian soil could not be treated with disdain. It took some time and some fighting before it became clear what kind of soldiers invaded Upper Canada and what they were worth in armed conflict. Unwilling to take any chances, the British army and the Canadian militia surrounded von Schoultz's 100 invaders with units numbering almost 2000 men.

The morning of Tuesday, November 13, 1838, brought about an artillery and musket duel between the Americans occupying well-prepared defensive positions and the surrounding Canadian units. Canadian militia losses rose quickly. The commanding officers, Colonels Plomer Young and Henry Dundas, decided to wait for artillery support.

The Americans were trapped. There was no hope of relief from the American side and no sign of any popular uprising sparked by the invasion force of "liberators." On the contrary, the strength of the surrounding Canadian militia grew day by day. Von Schoultz's forces grew weaker through losses and desertions. In five days the invasion was practically over, and the curtain fell on the spectacle observed from the American side of the river by those who had sent a young "Polish" officer on a mission to free the oppressed Canadians. Nils von Schoultz was taken prisoner and transported to Kingston to face a court martial.

The prisoner's defence was conducted by a young Kingston lawyer by the name of John A. Macdonald. He advised von Schoultz to rely on mitigating circumstances, but the commander of the invasion force decided to accept full responsibility for his actions. He acknowledged that he invaded Upper Canada acting on false assumption regarding the desires of the population, but he obstinately stood by his declaration that he was, in fact, guilty of an attack on a British colony and should be judged accordingly. The court had no alternative. Twelve members of the invading force were sentenced to death, and 60 to exile in Australia. Nils von Schoultz, pretending to the end that he was a Polish officer, was the only one executed and buried at the military base of Fort Henry. His comrades in arms met their end in a local district jail.

Nils Gustav von Schoultz never faltered in his declarations that he was a Polish officer. One may judge his actions emotionally, as a gallant romantic gesture, or cynically, as an attempt to hide the fact that he left a wife and two children so that he could seek new life in America, which would certainly tarnish his reputation as a tragic military hero. The legend of von Schoultz survived for over 100 years. The truth came out only when a descendant wrote his biography based on family documents.

In the meantime, von Schoultz entered Canadian history as a romantic Pole who continued in Canada

Nils Gustav von Schoultz

the noble fight for freedom, so unsuccessful in his native land. He was welcomed by Polish writers and Polish Canadians who were anxious to stress their presence in Canada and in our nation's history as early as possible. One hundred years after the battle of Windmill Point, on July 1, 1938, the anniversary of the events was celebrated near Prescott by, among others, the prime minister of Canada, William Lyon Mackenzie King and the Consul General of Poland in Ottawa, Jan Pawlica. A memorial plaque was placed to commemorate the Polish freedom fighter Nils Gustav von Schoultz, dead at the age of 41.

Although the truth was finally revealed, occasionally one may still find a statement to the effect that a Polish freedom fighter tried to liberate Upper Canada at Windmill Point and paid for the attempt with his life. Legends are notoriously hard to kill. We may, however, devote some time and effort to a reflection: why did Nils von Schoultz dress up in a mantle of Polish freedom fighter, and why did he persist in this deception? Was it only to hide his treatment of his family? Or was being Polish in early 19th-century Canada a key to respect and honour? Von Schoultz pretended to be someone he was not.

However, as eminent Canadian historian Peter Waite points out, the young Kingston lawyer who defended von Schoultz was impressed with the "Polish" freedom fighter. John A. Macdonald came to admire his client's character and toughness. According to Donald Creighton, Macdonald's noted biographer, the future prime minister of Canada referred to his experience with von Schoultz for the rest of his life. In future years, the same characteristic features demonstrated by von Schoultz—bravery, love of freedom, willingness to defend unpopular causes— were to be a trademark of the first prime minister of Canada. Thus, in an ironically indirect way, Polish people did influence the political future of Canada— even though they may not have been physically present.

CHAPTER TWO

LITTLE POLAND IN CANADA

Most major Canadian cities have their ethnic areas: Little Italy, Little Greece, Little Malta or Ethiopia. The map of Canada has been filled with names indicating the varied sources of immigration. Many towns, lakes, mountains and other geographical features of this vast land continue to bear the names given to them by the original inhabitants of the northern part of the continent, and many attest to France, England, Scotland or Ireland as the origin of their original population. As immigrants to Canada came from all over the world, there are also names of Icelandic (Gimli), Italian, German, Spanish (Rama) or even Hebrew (Thorah) origin. Canada was created by representatives of probably all of the nations in the world, including the Polish.

Ontario has its Little Poland in a remote area in the northeastern part of the province, which for a century and a half contained a small fragment of a European country transplanted over the ocean to Canadian soil. Transplanted and still growing well.

The Ontario region officially named Kaszuby came to life in 1858. A group of 18 families from the Kaszuby district in Poland settled there, along Opeongo settlement road, and the community became the first wholly Polish settlement in Canada. There were many such settlements and most of them survived to this day, creating the mosaic of modern-day Canada. What is unique about Kaszuby is its Polish character that has been maintained by fifth or sixth generation Canadians of Polish origin who still can and do speak the language of their forefathers. It is also worth noting that Polish immigrants settled on rocky, inhospitable land that did not attract others. The region promised hard work and little chance of success, compared to the more welcoming areas farther west. Polish settlers took what was being offered and raised the inhospitable land to Canadian standards.

Historians writing about 19th-century migration from Polish lands state at least two reasons these people searched for a new home on the other side of the Atlantic Ocean. The first is usually poverty—and no doubt the families who settled in Kaszuby came from a poor region of Poland. There is, however, another reason that made those people seek a new place in the world.

Poland in the 19th century was undergoing a period of lost independence. The national uprising of 1830 against the Russian rulers failed. The area of the country Prussia took over was not spared the consequences of this failed attempt at recreating Poland. The Prussian authorities started an anti-Polish campaign, which in the final years of the century resulted in attempts at forced assimilation of the Polish population into the German state. The assimilation had been enforced with typical Prussian precision—opponents were severely punished and practically placed outside the law.

In one of the legendary instances, a Polish peasant, Michał Drzymała, who lived in another region under Prussian occupation became a folk hero, and his story is well known by all Polish children. Drzymała was denied permission to build a house on his land because he was Polish. The law considered a shelter to be a house if it remained in the same place for more than 24 hours. Unfazed by legal obstacles, Drzymała purchased a circus wagon and moved his family there. The wagon was rolled to a different place every day, so it could not be considered a house, and Drzymała justly declared victory over persecution by Prussian legal eagles. Drzymała's wagon became a media hit, and a black eye for the Prussian authorities, but it did not serve as a precedent that could be adopted widely by the whole Polish peasantry under Prussian administration.

So the settlers of Kaszuby district came to Ontario, and, like their Irish counterparts, for example, were in search of economic opportunity and freedom to be themselves. The Kaszuby settlers' arrival is told in a Canadian Government Report of the Select Committee on Emigration of 1860:

> In 1858, 76 Poles (16 families) landed here by [a sailing ship] the Heinrich from Bremen. They had been told

by a passage agent for the Bremen shipping interest, that they would receive 100 acres of land on going to Canada, free of any expense or pay. They sold their little cottages and few acres, and landed here paupers. They had not as much as the value of a loaf of bread in money amongst them. They said the agent at home had deceived them, in telling them the cost of removal from Prussian Poland to Québec was a great deal less than they afterwards found out. These people were much more to be pitied, on account of their not speaking anything else but Polish. I shall never forget their bitter, despairing cries, when they found here on the other side of the ocean how awfully they had been misled. I procured free passages for them from the Chief Agent to Renfrew, and although late in the season I saw them all, except one family, for whom I could not get employment, provided for, with the farmers in that neighbourhood. They were considered a burthen on their arrival, but in one year they have already elicited honourable mention from the Ottawa Agency.

Canada offered the new settlers freedom to be Polish, and that may be the reason why the region is still referred to as a little stretch of Poland in Canada. Both "Poland" and "Canada" being equally important in this phrase.

Canadian immigration authorities had a particularly complex problem with Polish immigrants. Not only did they speak an outlandish-sounding language and spell their names in an incomprehensible manner, but they also usually insisted they came from a country that had not at that time existed on the map of Europe for almost 100 years. Thus, in immigration and settlement documents, the immigrants were described as

German or Galician (if they came from Austria), and their Polish nationality was often officially lost. To add to the confusion, there were two Galicias in Europe—one in today's Poland and the other in northwestern Spain. In the 19th century, neither enjoyed the status of an independent state recognized in the international arena. So where did these people come from?

Today, it is often difficult, and sometimes impossible to determine the true nationality of some immigrants to Canada collectively described as Ukrainians or Galicians, Germans or Austrians. Unless, like the descendants of Kaszuby settlers, they have preserved their national traditions and the remnants of their native language, which would leave no doubt that they are Polish.

Kaszebe Griffon—Canadian Kaszub coat of arms

Ironically, the Little Poland in Ontario was given the name of Kaszuby, a district of Poland inhabited by an ethnic group that spoke a distinct dialect of the Polish language and that today enjoys the status of a separate ethnic minority within the Polish nation. The Polish Kashub people have their own literature and their separate and individual characteristics of folk art. The inhabitants of Canadian Kaszuby, paradoxically, did not even realize they were a separate ethnic group. They were Poles, and that was it.

The records of settlement agent Thomas P. French show that the first Polish settlers in Renfrew County received their land sections on September 2, 1859. Some of those settlers included the names of Andrzej Kryszynski, Jozef Jezierski, Maciej Szczypior, Antoni, Mikołaj and Franciszek Princ. All together, 14 families or 57 persons received free land in Renfrew County. They came by boat to Farrell's Landing and then continued along Opeongo Road. At that time, the colonization road was more of a trail, hardly cleared enough to walk it. The group continued west, looking to the left and to the right to try to assess the worth of the land and how it would feed their families.

The land promised hard work. It was stony and the soil layer was relatively thin, which created problems for Thomas French, who could not understand why his pet project met with such little enthusiasm from the prospective settlers. It is clear that those who showed little interest in settling there were better equipped to assess the land's agricultural value. But what was most important for the Polish group was that the land was free for the taking, so they made their choices. A look at a modern map of Renfrew

County illustrates their decisions made over 150 years ago: Kulas Lake, Murak Flis Road, Shulist Lake, Lucovitch Road, Olsheski Road. The spelling of the landmarks has been anglicized over the years, but the names are unquestionably Polish in origin.

The land was covered with large stones and overgrown with primeval forest. Nevertheless, it presented the settlers with an opportunity to work and to cultivate their national pride. It also promised that they would be left in peace, without the necessity of looking for circus wagons. Thus, one of the settlements in this area still bears the name Hopefield—Field of Hope.

Polish peasantry was characterized by two factors: strong attachment to their nationality and language and an even stronger trust in the Roman Catholic faith. The Kashub settlers and their descendants retain both these characteristics today. Agent French was optimistic in his assessment of the success of his enterprise. He pointed out that his settlers spoke little English, but he was convinced they would prove to be good farmers and good citizens. Twenty years later, when the first post office was opened in Hagarty, the settlers decided to rechristen the location. Although they and their fathers came from the Baltic shores of Poland, for the new post office location they chose Wilno—the name of a Polish city located quite far from the Polish Kaszuby region. The name was chosen because it was the city of birth of their priest, Father Władysław Dembski.

The archbishop of Ottawa, Joseph T. Duhamel, recognized the Kashub settlers' right to spiritual care in the Polish language. On January 30, 1876, the first

Welcoming committee at Wilno in Kaszub folk costumes

Polish church was dedicated in Hagarty to Saint Stanisław Kostka, a 16th-century Polish Jesuit and patron of Poland. Unfortunately, the building was destroyed by fire in 1936.

In Barry's Bay, often simply called The Polish Town, there is a Catholic church dedicated to St. Jadwiga, a 15th-century Polish queen. One of the stained glass windows in the church bears the inscription "Boże zbaw Polskę" ("God Save Poland"). It was erected by Antoni Kulas, one of the descendants of the original settlers.

Today, most of the traces of the original settlement have disappeared, crumbled to dust. But not all. The Polish Kashub Heritage Museum and Skansen welcomes visitors interested in the traditions of Polish Kashub Ontarians. The museum was originally limited to displays in a small log building but has since become the main museum building with a resource library, a heritage store and heritage displays.

An official ribbon-cutting ceremony for the opening of Wilno Heritage Park and the Polish Kashub Heritage Museum was held on June 30, 2002, and that summer, Shirley Mask Connolly became the museum's first curator.

The park and open-air museum now includes three old-style log buildings, two smaller wooden buildings and a large timber frame machine shed. Inside the museum there are three displays: Remembering Our Polish Kashub Pioneers and Pioneer Days; Remembering Our Roots in Poland; and Remembering Our Men Who Fought for Poland and for Canada. The last display is mostly devoted to a little-known fact that Polish army units formed and trained on Canadian soil during the Great War.

Little Poland in Ontario is not only a historical, heritage trace of the Polish presence on the map of Canada, but it is also a living, inviting and attractive Polish episode in Canada's colourful multicultural history.

One of the modern-day attractions of the Kashub region is its rural character and the beauty of the hilly countryside filled with lakes. Ontario Kaszuby is a favourite "cottage country" retreat for many Polish Canadian families. It has also been deemed a perfect place for summer camps for young people, under the guidance of a lively youth organization known as the Polish Scouts. The Kaszuby region is the summer headquarters of an organization boasting hundreds of members in Ontario alone. Since the 1950s, young Polish Canadians have spent summers at three main troop bases around Barry's Bay, acquiring typical scouting skills, as well as learning a lot about their national roots and heritage.

One of my nephews, Paul, spent five consecutive summer months at Kaszuby, fascinated by sailing. He and his friends learned all they could sailing local lakes, and later broadened their knowledge at Toronto sailing clubs. Ten years later, Paul, a Canadian citizen, was given the command of a Polish yacht in the international regatta Tall Ships Race 2007 from Aarhus in Sweden to Kotka in Finland in the Baltic Sea. His training in Kaszuby paid off. Even though he commanded one of the oldest vessels in the competition, Paul and his Polish crew came close to winning in their class, with a Canadian flag flying from the mast of one of the Polish yachts in the race.

The years following World War II changed the character of Ontario's "Little Poland." The local population, which survived for almost 100 years eking out a living from this inhospitable terrain, started to gradually move out of Kaszuby in search of fortune in other regions of Canada. At the same time, Kaszuby began attracting Polish Canadians from Toronto, St. Catharines, Ottawa and Montréal. The first arrivals were the Boy Scouts. After them came lovers of the outdoors, who appreciated the wilderness, the fishing and the nature that was vaguely similar to their native Poland. Kaszuby retained its "Polish settlement" character but gained a reputation as the best Polish cottage country in Ontario.

Intensive tourist traffic required a post office. Its story explains how the name "Kaszuby" entered Canadian cartography. The first settlers did not consider themselves members of the Kashub ethnic minority and insisted they were simply Polish. They felt that the name "Kaszuby" was somehow offensive, as if excluding them from their true Polish nationality.

The idea of establishing another post office in the settlement, to supplement the offices in Wilno, Barry's Bay and Combermere for the convenience of the inhabitants of the region, came from Father Rafał Grzondziel, local priest and advocate of bringing young Canadians of Polish origin to his Catholic Youth Guidance Centre on Lake Wadsworth. Father Grzondziel came to be its first postmaster, and his post office was a desk in a barn near the chapel of Holy Mary Mother of Angels. The chapel was located at a point bearing the official name of Halfway, so named because it was located halfway between Combermere and Wilno.

Father Grzondziel disliked the name Halfway and stated his arguments in a letter written to the Canadian Board of Geographical Names. On June 14, 1960, he received a reply addressed to "Father Ignatius, Kaszuby, Ontario." The unofficial name became official, confirmed by the highest Canadian authority. The name "Kaszuby" is here to stay as a Polish reality in Canada.

Chapter Three

In Search of Land

Mass immigration of Poles to Canada began in the late 19th century. They came mostly from western and south-western Poland in search of arable land. They settled in Alberta, Saskatchewan and Manitoba, as those were the regions where land was available for homesteading. Many of them utilized their experience in mining to obtain jobs in Canada's coal industry. Some settlements, such as Coleman, Alberta, became for a period of time Polish towns. Today, the only recommended restaurant in Coleman is owned by a Polish Canadian and offers a menu of traditional Polish fare.

The estimates of Polish immigration to Canada in the period from 1895 to 1914 range from 50,000 to about 80,000 people. Most Poles came with their families and made attempts at homesteading, although in many cases their efforts failed because they lacked knowledge of the modern financial operations involved in maintaining an agricultural business. The Great War of 1914–18 interrupted immigration, but another wave swelled again after 1919.

The reasons the Poles left their country and came to Canada were two-fold. First, they were searching for a chance to improve their personal fortunes—just as all impoverished immigrants do, regardless of where they come from. The second reason was specific to the situation in their native country: reborn Poland experienced immense difficulties trying to rebuild the national economy from the three diverse areas administered for 150 years by Russia, Germany and Austria. The complexity of that problem escapes modern imagination: post–World War I Poland faced a task of coalescing its systems of civil law, three sets of economic institutions, three education systems and even three transportation networks, one of which ran on rails of a different gauge. And to complicate the matter further, the two-year-old state also faced the task of fighting a war against Soviet aggression in 1920.

Obviously, not every Polish person dreamt of undertaking these tasks, so many sought personal fortune on the other side of the Atlantic. All the more so, because by this time, Canada had become in Poland a symbol of prosperity, and the name of the country became synonymous with prosperity. The association of Canada with unimaginable riches was so strong that years later it surfaced in the most horrible circumstances— the sector of the Auschwitz-Birkenau Nazi death camp was called "Kanada," because that was the area where all the goods confiscated from the inmates were sorted, classified and packaged for transport to Germany.

Polish miner in Coleman, Alberta

Thus, some of the poorest peasants left their meagre huts in southern Poland, mainly in the province of Galicia, and sought land on the Canadian prairies. They were poor, uneducated, strange looking and usually spoke no English or any other language familiar to Canadians. Minister Clifford Sifton, the father of Canada's immigration policy, underestimated the reaction of the established Canadian population to the influx of such strangers. The Poles, like other immigrants from Eastern Europe, were often treated harshly and rejected by the residents of Alberta or Saskatchewan. At times, the situation required decisive action. In 1920, the relationship between the Poles and the local population in Camrose and Wetaskiwin in Alberta became unbearable. So much so that a defender came forward to speak for the Polish immigrants in the region—Father John Kulawy, a Polish missionary priest.

The English-speaking people said that Galicians (the common descriptive name for Poles and Ukrainians) were dirty, poor, had no homes (only holes in the soil) and had poor manners. Father Kulawy gave a speech sometime in the early 1900s in Camrose explaining the situation:

> The English-speaking people, especially those who came from the USA, build houses with borrowed money, live well and comfortably and do not work hard. But in a few years, they go broke and have to leave. In contrast, our people live in huts of clay because they came into this country with very little money. They are not afraid to work hard. They prefer to have no money than to borrow it. They came into this country to make money and, indeed, they make it. They stay on the land, they persevere, and they develop the land and work hard: for the welfare of their families and for Canada, their adopted fatherland. They would not leave their land; they would stay on it even if you would dare to drive them out. They would continue to cultivate it.

The stories of hardship suffered and overcome by the Polish settlers, both miners and homesteaders, are numerous, and today they generate wonder and respect. They are, however, quite similar to the stories of adversity and sacrifice, of harsh, merciless conditions and economic misfortune suffered and overcome by the settlers from other European countries, by

The family home of Michael Klish in Coleman, Alberta

Canadians from Eastern Canada and by migrants from all over the world.

Those who kept their noses to the grindstone survived and often prospered. Those who lacked strength, endurance, or sometimes, sheer luck, left defeated or died at the place that was supposed to be their land of milk and honey. A collection of memoirs called *Polish Settlers in Alberta* published by Polish Alliance Press in Toronto in 1979 contains many stories. One of them is a brief summary of the fortunes of Michael Klish, written by his daughter Anne Kolber.

My father, Michael Thomas Klish, was born in 1889, in Radziechowy, in south Poland. As a teenager he was apprenticed as a tailor, but he preferred to work in the coal mines. At the tender age of nineteen, he decided to

seek a better life in the new world. He arrived in Coleman, Alberta, in 1908, and was employed here by the
International Coal & Coke Company. He learned his English from the Welsh miners.

Whenever there was no demand for his services at
the mine, Klish worked as an apprentice carpenter and
participated in "building bees"—volunteer groups
that helped build homes for newcomers and friends.
In 1913, Klish married Rose Pieronek, and a few years
later tried his hand at farming, but soon returned to
Coleman. Rose died in the flu epidemic of 1919, so
the children had to be sent to their grand-parents'
farm in BC. They returned to Coleman in 1921, after
the death of their grandmother. Anne Kolber empha-
sizes the ties her father had with the Polish community
and his readiness to work with others for the common
good:

> Dad was a charter member of the Polish Society and
> helped build the present Polish Hall in Coleman. He was
> also on the committee which was instrumental in bring-
> ing electric power to East Coleman. In late 1942, after
> his daughters had left Coleman, he retired from the
> mine and moved to Calgary where he enjoyed his lei-
> sure years until his death in 1963.

There is a lesson to be learned from the stories of the
impoverished Polish settlers in the Prairie Provinces
when contrasted with the story of Cannington Manor
in Saskatchewan. The area is today a ghost town with
only traces of its former glory. In 1892, Captain
Edward Pierce established it as a model English colony
in the New World. Life in Cannington Manor

emulated the life of the British upper class, with thoroughbred racing, tennis, cricket, polo, fox hunting, theatrical plays and billiards. The settlers in the manor bred bulldogs and drank tea, while developing the land in their spare time. By 1900 the dream had died.

By contrast, the Canadian government paid each immigration agent in Europe $5 for talking a farmer into leaving his land and $2 to every member of the farmer's family. The investment proved much more profitable. The Poles, together with the Ukrainians, the Mennonites and countless others, were attracted to this "promised land." They started their lives in underground burrows, strained their muscles clearing the land and gambled on weather conditions and market vagaries. Some starved or left for greener pastures. Others survived to see the Prairie Provinces of today bloom and prosper. And they got to see their children and grandchildren live comfortably in a country that does not ask where you came from but only whether you are man or woman enough to stand up to its requirements.

How they accomplished this feat is depicted in a million stories. Each tale is different, and each is in fact the same: hard work, sacrifice, endurance and faith in themselves, in the country and in a merciful God. The story of the Polish settlers in the Prairies is best told through the story of three unusual brothers Jan (John), Wojciech and Paweł Kulawy.

The brothers were born in Leśnica, a small town in Silesia. Wojciech was the eldest, born on April 16, 1871, followed by Jan a year later.

Within 15 years, the family grew to include 10 children, with Paweł born as the fifth child in 1877.

They were poor, but not the poorest—the father's skill as a saddler, together with the income from a small farm, provided for the family and even made it possible for the two eldest brothers to continue their education in a college organized by the missionary order of Oblates of Mary Immaculate. Jan was the first to graduate and join the order formally on August 15, 1893. Together with his brother Wojciech, Jan was a missionary-trainee in the order's St. Joseph's Scholasticate in Ottawa. In 1894–95, both took their vows and started on their missionary career.

At that time, Paweł was already following in the footsteps of his older siblings and preparing for his own missionary life. His collegium superiors gave him particularly high marks for his academic and religious efforts. By 1902 all three brothers had taken their vows and were ready to serve the order.

By the turn of the 20th century, there already were about 20,000 Polish settlers and miners, mainly in Manitoba, with some families established in Saskatchewan and in the Alberta coal mines. Their need for spiritual guidance in their own language was becoming more evident, and the flow of immigrant priests from Europe was insufficient. Thus, the Catholic hierarchy turned to the missionary order for help. The first to travel west was Wojciech. In the fall of 1898 he visited Alberta, searching and finding Polish, Ukrainian and German Catholics in Canmore, Cochrane, Anthracite and Banff. All these settlements were just beginning to develop, so Father Kulawy had to organize Holy Mass in the most primitive conditions, often in the open air. Only his base in Winnipeg could boast of a real church where Mass could be held in Polish.

One year later Wojciech received help in his efforts from his brother Jan. They both travelled all over the prairies, systematically visiting numerous pockets of Polish immigrants, occasionally helping out with spiritual care in other, ethnically related communities. Often, this help meant performing tasks far from typical for a spiritual leader, such as assisting in an operation in a Canmore hospital, where the doctors tried to save the life of a Slovakian miner who lost a leg in a work-related accident.

"Our work takes care of three kinds of people: miners, railway workers and farmers," wrote Jan.

> Miners and railway workers live in easily accessible areas by the railway line, but it is a problem to gather them for a service, particularly during the week, when they cannot leave their jobs. Most of them are young, with families left behind in their country, to be sent for when they can afford it. They live without spiritual guidance for months on end and often stray away from organized religion. Farmers are more apt to keep the tradition brought over from their homeland. However, a priest trying to reach them must often travel 24, 30 or even 80 kilometres over roads which—in the event of rain—are practically impassable.

The two brothers travelled constantly from one settlement to another, performing all the Catholic rites whenever needed. They said Mass at private homes or in barns, they received confession, performed marriages, baptized newborn children and preached. Father Jan Kulawy noted in his memoirs that, fortunately, the hearts of his faithful were usually better prepared for receiving the rites of their faith than their houses were for receiving the priest. The visiting missionary did not have to announce his arrival. News of the impending visit spread like fire by word of mouth. It is no wonder that at a settlement of Ukrainians, he once baptized 20 children in one day. "I felt the same joy that was given to the Apostles, to see people coming so readily to the Church of Christ," wrote Father Jan Kulawy.

By 1899 it was evident that Winnipeg required a new Polish parish. It was temporarily housed in the Immaculate Conception parish in the city, but the first meeting organized by Fathers Wojciech and Jan Kulawy ended with a resolution to build a new church for the parish at Selkirk and Aikins Avenue in the northern part of the city. The decision was made in June 1899, and by November, Archbishop Adelard Langevin was able to say Mass in the new church. Its basement provided, for economic reasons, the living quarters for the two brothers.

Although the brothers were formally based in Winnipeg, they performed their duties all over the Prairie Provinces. Winnipeg, however, was special to them, not only because they lived there but also because the city allowed them to organize the first Polish parish school. Most of the children lacked any sort of education, which was typical in all Prairie settlements. For Catholic missionaries, as well as for most of their parishioners accustomed to religious education of their home country, public schools were inadequate and were often accused of leading the children away from their ethnic background and the faith of their fathers. In a few years the number of students in the parish school in Winnipeg reached 150 and it was necessary to move the school to a special building. The parish quickly grew with Father Jan Kulawy taking care of the Winnipeg Polish Catholics, while Wojciech spent most of his time travelling and serving the Polish settlements to the west.

Their work as travelling missionaries in difficult conditions of the Canadian West took its toll on their health. In 1904, Father Jan became ill and left for Europe, never to return to the parish he organized. A year later Wojciech followed in his path, moving to Philadelphia, and later returning to Poland. Their place in the Prairies was taken over by the third Kulawy brother, Paweł.

Father Paweł Kulawy was the first Polish oblate missionary to settle permanently in Alberta. He worked in the province for 18 years, earning the respect and admiration of his Polish parishioners. Originally based in Lethbridge, he soon moved to Calgary but spent

Father Paweł Kulawy

most of his time travelling all over the province, wherever his services were needed by Polish-speaking Catholics. He was instrumental in building a Catholic church in Coleman and became a regular visitor to Camrose, Calgary, Edmonton, Rabbit Hills, Round Hill and Kopernick.

In 1906 Father Paweł Kulawy moved to Round Hill to better serve his community concentrated in that area of the province, even though it meant sharing his work time with the profession of a farmer. The community was too poor to procure a local parish priest, so Father Paweł acquired a small farm to supplement the church's income.

Commenting on the problems in his work, Father Kulawy pointed out that a travelling priest often has to cover enormous distances over inadequate roads. Particularly in an Alberta winter, travelling as far as 40 kilometres to perform a service in a church in Kopernick presented a challenge. Once the winter storm was so severe that even the horses lost their sense of direction and Father Kulawy found himself, after a couple of hours of travel, back where he started. This did not stop the missionary; he tried again, and he reached his faithful parishioners at 2:00 AM. The regular Sunday service was held as usual.

Years later in Poland, Father Kulawy commented that if he was to send a priest to work in such conditions as he himself experienced in Alberta, he would never allow it. He stayed in the province for almost two decades, however, and his work left an indelible imprint. One of his main concerns was education, and today a school district in Alberta bears his name.

Most of the tasks Father Paweł Kulawy performed in Alberta were connected with his mission. But he also assisted his flock in whatever he was asked to. In Calgary, he organized collections for his parishioners in rural areas, and he helped in legal matters whenever his parishioners encountered problems because of their insufficient command of English. Like his elder brother Jan, Paweł tried to accelerate the process of acceptance of his countrymen by Alberta society.

When the Polish settlers moved from the Round Hill area to Edmonton, Father Kulawy followed them to serve their needs, together with Father Antoni Sylla, another Polish priest who had worked in Banff and the surrounding area since 1909. By 1920 the Polish Catholic environment in Alberta was well developed, with parishes, churches and schools. The settlers themselves became successful and prospered, thanks to the hard work of the missionaries. But still, it meant that Father Paweł Kulawy had to regularly travel to perform his duties in Rabbit Hills, Kopernick, Mundare and Chipman.

His work in Canada ended in 1921 when he went back to his native Poland, originally for a short leave. His return to Alberta was the subject of correspondence between the Catholic order in Rome and Bishop Emile Legal, who demanded, in the strongest terms possible, that Father Kulawy return to Alberta. Father Paweł Kulawy wanted to come back to Canada, and he wrote a letter to that effect to the order authorities in Rome. The decision to keep him in Poland proved final. All three brothers met once again in their native country.

They continued their work with the order in Europe. Father Jan Kulawy visited Canada in 1924 to celebrate the 25th anniversary of establishing the Holy Ghost Parish in Winnipeg. During World War II, both Jan and Paweł Kulawy, although formally Canadian citizens, were arrested by the Nazi secret police, the Gestapo. Father Paweł Kulawy died on August 21, 1941, in the Nazi death camp in Auschwitz-Birkenau. Three weeks later, his brother Jan followed him. Their elder brother Wojciech learned of their fate but survived them by only a few months. The location of their graves in unknown. The monuments reminding the Catholic population of their work can be found in many places in western Canada.

It is difficult to imagine the hardships that faced the immigrants to western Canada at the turn of the 20th century. Some insight may be gained from literature, as for example, from the novels of Frederick P. Grove. In 1950 one of the best Polish reporters, Melchior Wańkowicz, travelled through the Prairie Provinces gathering material for his semi-documentary novel *Tworzywo* (Fabric). He composed the book around four fictionalized biographies of Polish immigrants to Saskatchewan and Alberta. Today, it reads like a horror story, narrating unimaginable hardships and difficulties these people faced in their struggle for existence.

The history of Polish settlers in the prairie provinces of Canada follows the pattern detectable in other ethnic communities. The Poles, however, had to deal with some additional problems, such as difficulties in communication or estrangement from the community. At the same time, they enjoyed some advantages—they were used to poverty and hard work and were equipped with rich traditional knowledge of agriculture and accustomed to making a living off the land. The novels of Grove and Wańkowicz give modern Canadians an insight into the scale of adversity that their ancestors dealt with and is a recipe for personal and communal success.

Stefan Czołowski was one of the first to arrive in western Canada. His story, as recorded by Tadeusz Walkowski, reads in part:

> Stefan Czołowski was born on August 4, 1875, in the little Polish village of Wolczucha, near Gródek Jagiellon-ski. He attended high school in Lwów until the death of his father, an insurgent of 1863, and later, a participant in the movement for better education. Stefan was forced to quit school, take over the family farm, and bring up his is brothers and sisters.

In July 1897, Czołowski came to Edmonton. He had little money and no knowledge of English, but he managed to find employment at a local farm. His pay was $12 per month. Czołowski worked from dawn to dusk, but the job was also an opportunity to learn English. He made excellent progress and soon was able to help other Slavic immigrants in communicating with the English Canadian settlers and officials in Edmonton.

With practice obtained in a series of odd jobs, Czołowski gained enough experience to try his hand at farming. He bought himself a quarter section of land near Bruderheim and started farming on his own, together with his new wife. Walkowski records further:

He farmed with great zeal and love for the soil. Soon he was considered a model farmer, and became an advisor to the people in his community, in matters of farming, political and social interest. He also held a position in municipal affairs, elected by many ethnic groups in his region…. As a great horse lover (he once served in the Austrian cavalry), he ran a model breeding program on his farm. His military background showed in his orderliness in the stables. With the advent of mechanization, and much regret, Stefan Czołowski had to switch from horses to machines, but he still maintained a few horses on his farm. The cavalry tradition could not be forgotten.

After 50 years of hard work, Czołowski and his wife retired to Lamont, Alberta. They led an active social life, often hosting their countrymen and members of their family, which by 1951 numbered over 100 people. They raised five daughters and eight sons.

Another immigrant story of Charles Mamczasz was narrated by a daughter of the settler, L.F. Frantz, and published by Joanna Matejko in the book *Reminiscences and Biographies*. Mamczasz's daughter said:

My father, Charles (Karol) Mamczasz, was born November 5, 1889, at Ostrów (Sokal) in Galicia. His parents were farm workers, and as a young man in Poland he worked in a brick factory. He did not have any formal school education, but did extra work to earn money in order to obtain some private lessons.

The young man heard about the possibilities of making a new living in the prosperous country of Canada and decided to do what others did before him—save money for a boat ticket and search for his fortune far

First bridge built by Charles (Karol) Mamczasz, Polish contractor, Carrot River, Saskatchewan, 1938

away from his homeland. He travelled alone, with little information and directions, but finally, in 1911, he arrived in Canada and went from Montréal to Prince Albert, Saskatchewan.

"His first job was working at Burns & Company, butchering cattle, at a wage of about 35 cents per hour," continued Mamczasz's daughter. "He initially lived in a small house with another young man who also worked at Burns. At first he spoke only Polish and Ukrainian, but as he worked longer, he learned to speak, read and write in English."

Immigration to Canada was at that time a personal enterprise, and Mamczasz, like other immigrants, received little help from the federal or provincial authorities in settling. Assistance was a personal matter, and Charlie (as his friends called him) in turn helped others come to Canada and establish a foothold in their new country. Soon, Canada was home to his parents, brothers, sisters, other relatives and friends.

In November 1918, Charles Mamczasz married Mary Billay. Two daughters and a son were subsequently born of this union.

Having acquired some experience, Mamczasz started his own business, Mamczasz Construction Co., which was active in the field of road construction and bridge building. The company built a bridge across the Carrot River in Saskatchewan, then near Prince Albert and Shellbrook. He continued working till the 1950s, when he sold part of the business to his son. Although he was by this time aged 65, he did not relish retirement; he moved to Calgary and continued building bridges and other road installations in Alberta, Saskatchewan and Manitoba until 1971.

> He was a deeply religious man. He belonged to the Knights of Columbus, Prince Albert Council, and was a member of the initial committee that worked to establish the Polish Parish in Calgary. The construction of the Queen of Peace Church was completed on April 20, 1968.... Charlie enjoyed his life, liked to talk to people, and always had a happy smile on his face.

Although Alberta and Saskatchewan provided homes to many settlers from Poland, the true home away from home for a majority of new Canadians from that part of Europe was in Manitoba. Statistical data regarding the nationality of the settlers of Canadian West is notoriously unreliable because of the difficulty in establishing the nationality of Eastern European immigrants. However, even taking this into account, it is estimated that before 1911, over 13,000 immigrants from Poland came to Canada, to settle mainly in Ontario and on the Prairies.

Alberta welcomed almost 2000, Saskatchewan almost 2400, but Manitoba became the Promised Land for almost 4500 Poles—about one-third of the total for the whole of Canada. In the 1910s and 1920s, the primary centre of Polish settlement was in Ontario, but Manitoba still took in about 20 percent of Polish immigrants. As mentioned earlier, the Polish names in today's Manitoba are associated with the unfortunate experiment of Lord Selkirk.

The first Polish name writ large in the history of today's Manitoba belonged to Edwin Brokovski, the son of Augustus Brokovski, who was a nobleman and officer of the Polish army and one of the thousands of people forced into exile by the disaster of the 1830 uprising against tsarist Russia. Edwin Brokovski was in fact only half-Polish: his mother was English, and he was born and brought up in England before immigrating to Canada at age 19. However, we can justifiably include him in a story of Poles in Manitoba; after all, his son J. Craig Brokovski published a brief study of the history of his family in 1940 under the title *I Am Proud of My Name.*

Edwin received an excellent education (his parents met while studying music with Franz Schubert), and his first job in Canada was far from the usual lot of an immigrant—he was given a teaching position. During his initial stay in Toronto, he joined a volunteer rifle company and later did some service defending Canada during the Fenian raids. Two years later he moved to Winnipeg to work as a surveyor. There he purchased the *Manitoba Gazette and Trade Review*, and when the paper closed, he continued to work as a reporter.

Edwin Brokovski was an active member of the community. He helped to organize the local rifle association and the Manitoba Board of Trade, and he was actively involved in local artistic life. He spent his summers in Toronto promoting the idea of settling in Manitoba. His contribution to the development of the new areas of Canada was appreciated—in 1884, living at that time in Ontario, he was appointed justice of the peace and notary public for North-West Territories. Brokovski was considered to be "a good soul, helpful in every possible way." At age 72, he filed for a homestead in the Prongua district and continued as a notary and justice of the peace and maintained his interest in military activities, leading the veterans' church parade in 1913.

Brokovski has been described as one of the most eminent Polish figures in Canada, and he instilled in his eldest son, John Craig, an enduring sense of Polish identity. Edwin Brokovski was not, however, a typical representative of the Polish immigration to Canada or Manitoba in the 19th century. His compatriots came to their new homeland without all the assets he possessed. Uneducated, without any knowledge of English, often lost in their new surroundings and short of help from an unsympathetic local population, the Poles settling in Manitoba faced an uphill battle— maybe even a little more uphill than what an average immigrant faced. What is more, Polish immigration to Canada at that time differed substantially from the process experienced by other ethnic groups.

Unlike Germans, Finns, Icelanders or Ukrainians (thanks to Professor O. Oleskow), the Poles arriving in Manitoba at the turn of the 19th century were unorganized. Neither in Canada nor in Poland was there a systematic effort at settling the immigrants in a specific area, even in a semi-organized manner. The Poles arrived in Canada individually, often without their families, who followed later at their own risk and usually without any plan as to where to settle. Other ethnic groups enjoyed a little (or a lot) more planning in their move to the new land. The Poles were left, by Canada, and by their native land, to their own devices. Thus, they followed the pattern of immigration by infiltration, rather than planned settlement.

Lack of organized Polish settlements made the settlers' job somewhat difficult, but at the same time, bore unexpected fruit. Most of the Poles settling in Manitoba came in contact with Ukrainian settlers. Fellow Slavs were a welcome sign: at least the two groups had no major problem in communicating because the Polish and Ukrainian languages are closely related. With time, the ties between the Polish and their much more numerous Ukrainian neighbours became even closer, the two communities enjoying not only ease of communication but also the closeness of faith.

Ukrainians, like the Poles, are predominantly Catholic, even though they follow the Eastern rite in their liturgy. This proximity in fact and in spirit resulted in a distinct feeling of closeness between the two peoples. "We" is the term these settlers used to designate their communities, whether Polish or of Ukrainian in composition. And this was at a time when the relationship between these two nations back in their European homeland systematically worsened.

Polish Canadian historian Victor Turek comments on the relationship in his definitive book *Poles in Manitoba:*

> The Ukrainians assisted the Poles in tilling the soil, cutting down forests, draining swamps, and making roads. And the Poles helped them in similar tasks. This cooperation was so close, and conditions of living so interrelated that we find it exceedingly difficult to separate the Polish achievements from those partly, or entirely Ukrainian, when surveying the results of the pioneer effort of the Poles in Manitoba from a distance of half a century.

How close was this Polish Ukrainian integration "Made in Canada"? Geographers battle over the origin of place names in the newly settled land, interpreting this process as a sign of familiarizing the strange circumstances one finds oneself in. Manitoba is full of Slavic place names—are they Polish or Ukrainian? In most cases, it is impossible to tell. Without a specific and verbalized plan, without manifestos and declarations of friendship between nations, without much philosophy or politics, the Poles and the Ukrainians undertook the task of building a Canada that was free of some of the ideological baggage from across the ocean. It's no wonder then that decades later, a Polish Member of Parliament, Dr. Stanley Haidasz, became Canada's first Minister of State for Multiculturalism.

CHAPTER FOUR

PLEASE HELP WITH THE WAR

World War II brought a dramatic change to the Polish immigration to Canada. Gone were lines of uneducated, often illiterate peasant families. Taking their place were well-educated and fully qualified technicians, engineers and veterans of the Polish armed forces, often with almost six years of combat experience. They were to continue the tradition and build on the achievements of Kazimierz Gzowski, August Globensky (a physician and pharmacist who lived in Verchers, Québec, from 1791 to 1830), cartographer and surveyor Charles (Karol) Blaskowitz, and civil engineer, seigneur and politician Alexandre Kierzkowski, among others.

After the September Campaign of 1939, many Polish engineers and technicians took refuge, mainly in the United Kingdom, with some settling down in the unoccupied areas of France. At the same time, Canada embarked upon rapid development of its defence industry, and it needed a qualified technical workforce.

During his visit to London, England, C.D. Howe, the Canadian Minister of Munitions and Supply, examined the option of inviting Polish professionals to Canada. Soon after, an agreement with the Polish government in exile was concluded, allowing several Polish engineers and technicians to come to Canada on temporary visas. Most of them, however, were destined to stay in Canada permanently. They were needed, and they proved their qualifications.

One of the first Polish engineers to come to help Canada deal with wartime production was Czesław Peter Brzozowicz. Born in 1911, he graduated in civil engineering from a renowned university of Lwów in 1939, only to start his professional career by serving for three years in the Polish army in Poland and France. In Canada, his first job was surveying terrain for highways in British Columbia. In 1944, he designed northern Ontario plants for Marathon Paper Mills. When the war ended, he foresaw the coming boom and established a consulting engineering firm. His first client was Canadian Breweries Ltd.

As the author of his obituary wrote decades later in *The Globe and Mail:*

> Brzozowicz made a name for himself designing concrete structures reinforced with imbedded steel bars. It was a relatively uncommon practice in Canada, since the short construction season was considered unfavourable for poured concrete walls. Gruff and insistent,

Peter was on the ground floor of an engineering trend
that would become enormously popular.

It may well be said that Brzozowicz's imprints on the
Canadian landscape were indelible. He was one of
the consultants who helped construct the first subway
line in Toronto and was instrumental in the process of
constructing the tallest building in the Commonwealth in the 1960s, the Toronto-Dominion Centre
designed by Mies van Rohe.

Brzozowicz's obituary underlines that his expertise
was also of great value to the designers of the world's
first tower with a revolving restaurant, the Skylon
Tower in Niagara Falls. The tower was something of
a dress rehearsal for the latter, more ambitious project:
the CN Tower in Toronto. Brzozowicz played an
important role in making sure the world's tallest free-
standing structure had solid foundations.

"Brzozowicz was a structural engineer and visionary
who brought sound engineering practices to a young
nation not yet known for its building environment.
Like many newcomers, he arrived in Canada with
a few dollars, his professional training and an inex-
haustible appetite for work.... A graduate of the old
school, Peter believed anything was possible if you
studied and worked hard," the author of his obituary
also wrote.

Brzozowicz was not the only Pole who helped to
build Canada. In 1940, a group of about 50 Polish
engineers found themselves in Canada, mostly in
Toronto, Ottawa and Montréal, helping with the
building of the Canadian economic war machine. Initially, Canadians were distrustful of the Polish

engineers. It was difficult to imagine that professionals from the same country that had only recently sent illiterate peasants could perform tasks requiring knowledge, experience and talent. For Canadian industrialists, the concept of "a Polish engineer" was foreign: his abilities and trustworthiness were suspect.

"Trying to find the first job for Mr. Szwarc, I contacted 83 firms," wrote Ryszard Herget, appointed to the Bureau of Technical Personnel in the Ministry of Labour in Ottawa.

> This was a record. If not a world record then surely a Canadian one. Our second record holder was our president, Mr. Pawlikowski. When, after a lengthy wait, Mr. Szwarc finally got to the feed-bag, in a short time he became an indispensable employee of the biggest pulp and paper concerns, and eventually became the technical director of one of the corporation's plants. Dr. Pawlikowski, in time, became a professor at the École Polytechnique, and afterwards, a highly renowned associate of the technical branch of the municipal government of the city of Montréal.

Thus, one of the first tasks Polish engineers faced was to convince Canadians they were up to the job. That was why, in the spring of 1941, Polish engineers decided to organize the Association of Polish Technicians, which was to be a Canadian chapter of a professional organization in their homeland. The founding members formulated two aims of the organization: to help Polish engineers find their place in Canada, and to bring in more of their colleagues who had been dispersed all over the world by the war.

These technicians made it to safe Canadian shores out of occupied France, through Spain and Portugal, sometimes with the help of U.S. authorities who issued them visas and were well aware of the final destination of the specialists. The stories of these engineers read like a thriller novel. Regretfully, no one has bothered to write them.

Altogether, during World War II, Canada accepted about 800 Polish refugees. Families of high-level members of Polish administration constituted about one-quarter of that number; the rest were engineers, technicians and experts of the defence industry. Their stay in Canada was to be provisional—until the end of the war. Most of them, however, were later given the status of Canadian Resident.

Appreciation for the efforts of Polish engineers was possibly best expressed in a letter from the Secretary General of the Engineering Institute of Canada, L.A. Wright, to the Department of Immigration:

> Until now we have thought that German engineers were the most highly qualified technically in Europe. But after becoming familiar with the work of the Polish engineers within our industries, we have changed our minds, since we verified that in many instances they are superior to their German colleagues.

How important were Polish engineers and other specialists to Canada, its industry and economy and the war effort? The biographies below illustrate some of these men's contributions.

Mieczysław Gregory Bekker was a Polish engineer and scientist, a graduate of Warsaw Technical University class of 1929. He worked for the Polish Ministry of Military Affairs at the Army Research Institute in Warsaw on systems for tracked vehicles to work on uneven ground. In 1942 he accepted the offer of the Canadian government to move to Ottawa to work in armoured vehicle research. He entered the Canadian army a year later and reached the rank of lieutenant colonel.

Bekker was a leading specialist in the theory and design of military and off-the-road locomotion vehicles, and his work was of great importance in the development of the Canadian military vehicle industry. Bekker's work in Canada led to the publication in 1956 of the book *Theory of Land Locomotion*, considered a groundbreaking theoretical basis for a new engineering discipline called terramechanics. Bekker may well be regarded as the man who ensured future success of Canadian armoured vehicle design and production.

In 1951 Bekker moved to the U.S. to become research professor at the Stevens Institute of Technology, in Hoboken, New Jersey, and at the University of Michigan in Ann Arbor. He was the founder and the first director of the U.S. Army's Land Locomotion Laboratory in Detroit and the designer—at the General Motors A.C. Defense Research Laboratory in Santa Barbara, California—of the first extraterrestrial passenger surface vehicle, the lunar rover.

Bekker authored the general idea and contributed significantly to the design and construction of the lunar roving vehicle used by the missions of *Apollo 15*,

Apollo 16 and *Apollo 17* on the moon. He was the author of several patented inventions in the area of off-the-road vehicles, including those for extraterrestrial use. In May 1975, Bekker was awarded an honorary degree of Doctor of Engineering, by Carleton University in Ottawa "...in recognition of his outstanding contribution to transportation engineering...."

Commenting on the development of the first lunar rover on the moon, Bekker said, "First of all I realized that many years of my work have not been wasted. It was a fascinating adventure, and there are times when I find it difficult to comprehend the sequence of events which lead to my participation in it...."

Bekker reminds us that Jules Verne's heroes and those of other science fiction authors always walked on the moon, they never drove. Coincidentally, only one Polish writer, Jerzy Żuławski, in his novel *On the Silver Globe* (published in 1911), visualized a "lunar car," a vision that, 60 years later, became a reality thanks to the efforts of Mieczysław Bekker.

Dr. Teodor J. Błachut arrived in Canada from Switzerland in 1951 by invitation from the National Research Council (NRC) to organize its photogrammetric research section. Photogrammetric mapping is a methodology by which precision flown aerial photographs, accurate camera and ground control data are combined with digital data capture to produce planimetric and topographic maps. The section organized by Błachut has since become one of the leading photogrammetric research centres in the world, and many important methods and novel photogrammetric instruments trace their origins there. Błachut held several patents on instruments that he invented. The long list of achievements of the Photogrammetric Research Section organized by Błachut includes, among others, the development of the photogrammetric analytical plotter, the creation of software for analytical photogrammetry and the development of the stereo-orthophoto approach for three-dimensional mapping.

In addition to his scientific work, Błachut was active in Canadian, American, Pan-American and international learned societies, where he occupied numerous leadership positions. In 1970, he was elected a fellow of the Academy of Science of the Royal Society of Canada. He wrote over 130 publications and several books on geodetic, photogrammetric and cartographic subjects that were published in English, French, Spanish, Polish, German, Chinese and Japanese. In 1988, the United Nations Economic Commission for Africa invited him to carry out extensive studies in eastern and southeastern subregions of Africa to formulate a basic program of integrated general land information systems. Dr. Błachut died in 2004.

Dr. R. Gajda joined the Department of Mines and Technical Survey in Ottawa in 1943, and his knowledge and drive quickly gained him the position of chief of cartography in the geographical branch of the department. Gajda specialized in Canadian arctic surveys and research. He was involved with exploratory missions that, in 1948–51, were sent to the Arctic and

Western Greenland jointly by Canada and the United States. For many years, Gajda spent several summer months in the Arctic in areas that could only be reached by air. He was considered an expert on the Arctic and wrote several papers about the region. Gajda also created one of the first three-dimensional maps of Canada.

Stan Cyma received the Polish Civil Award for long and outstanding service in the aircraft industry. Cyma, like the majority of Polish aeronautical engineers during World War II, left Poland on the orders of the Polish government and went to France. In France he was directed to go to the Devitine Aircraft factory as the group leader of several Polish specialists. After the collapse of France, Cyma went to England, and in February 1941, left for Canada to work in the wartime industry. He joined the National Steel Car Company Ltd. in 1942, and from there, transferred to Victory Aircraft Ltd. and finally to A.V. Roe Ltd. (commonly known as Avro Canada) in Malton, Ontario, where he was responsible for planning the company's many facilities.

At Avro, Cyma was eventually entrusted with the position of Chief Plant Engineer in charge of the Plant Engineering and Development Offices, Maintenance Shop, Fire Protection and Plant Services. He also was a team leader of the Polish engineers working there. These engineers included B. Baranowski, E. Baranowski, Z.M. Fabierkiewicz, R. Sulatycki and E. Zobel.

When Wacław Czerwiński, renowned designer and constructor of gliders, first arrived in Canada in 1941, he was almost immediately appointed a group leader and a project engineer with DeHavilland Aircraft of Canada Ltd. in Downsview, Ontario. The company worked on the redesign of a wooden airplane, the famous Mosquito, a long-range fighter-bomber, to adapt it to American engines. In 1943, Czerwiński resigned from DeHavilland to become chief engineer and co-owner of Canadian Wooden Aircraft Ltd.

After World War II, he joined A.V. Roe Ltd. as a member of the designers' team for the Canadian fighter plane, the famous Avro Arrow. After the cancellation of the Arrow program, Czerwiński joined the aerodynamics section of the National Research Council in Ottawa, and later the Institute of Aerospace Sciences at the University of Toronto. From 1946 to 1959 he was a special lecturer at the University of Toronto aerodynamical department.

The wartime production success of DeHavilland owed a lot to Polish engineers. Together with Wacław Czerwiński there worked another experienced Polish aircraft designer named W.J. Jakimiuk. He was recognized as a brilliant aircraft designer even before World War II, not only in Poland but also abroad. After his arrival in Toronto in 1940, he was appointed to the position of chief of engineering at DeHavilland to work on the redesign of the Mosquito. By the end of the war, DeHavilland of Canada started to prepare for peacetime production, and Jakimiuk was the leader in the design and construction of two more aircraft. Jakimiuk, together with Mr. W. Stępniewski and other Poles, built the Chipmunk and the Beaver.

The Chipmunk was a small plane, suitable for flying in the harsh conditions of the Canadian North. Foreseeing the need for a larger aircraft, the team started preliminary studies of the Beaver. Stępniewski left for the U.S., but the design, under Jakimiuk, was completed. The Beaver was and still is a famous and popular bush plane. The design concepts and approach used for the Chipmunk and the Beaver allowed DeHavilland to progress with other types of aircraft to reach its Short Take Off and Landing (STOL) line of aircraft, which is popular all over the world.

Before World War II, G.W. Jankowski worked as a designer and developer of air brakes for freight trains. In 1942, he immigrated to Canada, and from 1943 he worked on various kinds of heavy equipment for the Bridge and Tank Company of Canada Ltd. In a relatively short time, Jankowski attained the position of senior mechanical engineer. He stayed with the company until his retirement and then became involved in numerous consulting assignments, mostly regarding machinery for movable bridges, heavy equipment for navigable waterways, cranes and hydraulic-lift installations for the maintenance of subway trains for the Toronto Transportation Commission as well as other similar projects.

As a consulting engineer, Jankowski cooperated on the construction of several projects for the St. Lawrence

Seaway Authority: two rolling lift bridges (Iroquois and Cote St. Catherine), the Beauharnois swing bridge, the Port Dalhousie swing bridge and the operating machinery for the Burlington Canal lift bridge.

Dr. Adam Jaworski arrived in Canada after World War II, following distinguished service in the 303 Polish Fighter Squadron (famous for the number of German fighters shot down during the Battle of Britain). His first position in Canada was at the National Research Council as an engine specialist. He later moved to the Economic Policy and Research Branch of the Department of Transport in Ottawa, where he was responsible for the fiscal policy of the aviation branch.

Jaworski repeatedly recommended landing fees for planes on Canadian airfields, but his most important achievement was calculating the "Canadian space rentals" for most of the airlines. The federal government accepted his position that all the foreign airlines using Canadian space, as well as that of Canadian radar, radio and other navigational facilities, should pay rental fees.

It should be noted that Canada is the shortest distance between Europe and the eastern United States on the "great circle route," and thus Canada was frequently part of a trans-Atlantic journey. All the airlines agreed to pay the tariff, a source of considerable income to the federal government of Canada, with American Airlines being the last airline to comply.

You can find Polish names on the payroll of almost all important companies and institutions of wartime and post-war Canada. One of the three architects who designed the Canada Pavilion at Expo '67 was Z. Stankiewicz. And one of the most indispensable specialists and innovators in Canadian paper industry was A. Szwarc, the inventor of water- and vapour-resistant paper coating. His son George wrote:

> My father Alexander Szwarc was born in Zgierz in 1899. He graduated from Poznan University with a PhD in Chemistry. He fought as a corporal in the First World War and as a major in the Cavalry in the Second World War. He was captured by the Russians, escaped from a military concentration camp and by way of Lithuania, Latvia, Estonia, Sweden managed to escape to France to rejoin the Polish Army.... We...came to Canada as immigrants in 1941, settling in Montréal. My father had several jobs in the pulp-paper and plastics industries. At about the age of 55 he ventured out to do some consulting and retired at 65. He died at the age of 89 in Montréal...

Often, Polish specialists were offered positions of responsibility and held them with impressive results. The following list is a small sample of some of the companies that have employed Polish experts:

3M: R. Nowakowski, who built the first 3M factory in France and the second one in Germany. He was subsequently appointed director of engineering of 3M in Europe.

Bell Telephone Company of Canada Ltd.: Z. Krupski in 1961 was appointed chief engineer and in 1964 chairman of the Trans-Canada Telephone

System, which was instrumental in completion of the main microwave communication system of the company.

Canadian Car Foundry Company in Montréal, Aircraft Division: Eryk Kosko was the author of stress calculations of modifications to several aircraft, was an earlier professor of aircraft design at École Polytechnique de Montréal and then a long-time research officer at the National Research Council in Ottawa as well as author of "Vibration Analysis of ANIK Satellite Structure."

National Aeronautical Establishment: Kazimierz Orlik-Ruckeman was a Fellow of the Canadian Aeronautical and Space Institute (CASI) and a Fellow of the American Institute of Aeronautics and Astronautics (AIAA). He was also the author or co-author of some 130 scientific papers and reports; he lectured in 16 countries, was co-inventor of the "Dampometer" that revolutionized free-oscillation experiments and could be found in most of the major aeronautical laboratories in the Western world, and was a consultant to NASA and NATO

Ontario Hydro: W. Krajewski was with the company since 1948 and was in charge of the design of the Lakeview, Lambton, Nanticoke, Lennox and Wesleyville generating plants.

BIRTH OF COMPUTING DEVICES OF CANADA

During World War II, the Polish Government in Exile considered establishing a Polish aircraft factory in England or in Canada, managed by Poles, because many engineers and technicians from the Polish aircraft industry managed to escape from Poland after the start of the war, ending up in England and Canada. After long negotiations and consultations, the plan was found to be impractical and was abandoned. However, the Polish spirit of enterprise and risk-taking didn't allow the specialists and talented engineers and technician to give up. Instead of establishing an aircraft factory in England, they came to Canada to help create and develop many industries in their new country.

Although a vast majority of Polish engineers decided to work for Canadian companies, several started their own companies. One of the most successful and important to Canada "Polish" firms was Computing Devices of Canada, established by two Poles, Dr. George Gliński and J. Norton-Spychalski, and a Canadian investor P.E. Mahoney.

Dr. G. Gliński arrived in Canada in 1943 from occupied France by the "normal route" travelled by displaced Poles: Spain, Portugal, Mexico and finally Canada. He started to work for General Electric (GE) in the research division. In 1948, he was approached by J. Spychalski and P.E. Mahony to join Computing Devices of Canada as a partner and director of the development division. A few months later, still working at the Computing Devices and teaching at McGill, Dr. Gliński was contacted by the University of Ottawa to organize from scratch a department of electronics. Gliński did this in record time, and soon the department acquired a deservedly good name in Canada, with Gliński as its chairman, a position that he held until his death. In memory of his contribution, since 1964, the university faculty annual award for excellence in scientific research is called the George Glinski

Award, and Glinski Drive was named in his honour, located in the heart of Ottawa University.

In the 1960s, practically all military aircraft in Canada and most of the aircraft in Europe carried some sort of instrument or other electronic equipment designed and manufactured by Computing Devices. Several companies in Europe manufactured the company's famous Position and Homing Indicator (PHI, which indicated the position of the aircraft in the horizontal plane).

Keith Smillie, professor emeritus of computing science at the University of Alberta in Edmonton, reminisces:

> One very large contract which had a significant influence on the company's growth was for the Kicksorter, a digital pulse counter designed at the Chalk River Laboratories of Atomic Energy of Canada Limited. If the Kicksorter had been slightly modified to do simple arithmetic, it would have been a rudimentary computer. A large number of these devices were purchased by AECL from 1957 until 1963.

Computing Devices products were manufactured under licence in France, Italy, Germany and England. In Ottawa at the end of the 1950s, the company employed well over 2000 people, of whom a large percentage were scientists and engineers.

Computing Devices' beginnings were modest, however. In 1948, the company consisted of only nine people when it received a study order from the Canadian Navy for the Tactical Trainer; that is, to study the possibility of training naval officers in war games in the laboratory. Eight years of work and more than

6000 tubes and tons of steel frameworks went into the design and construction of the massive computer, controls and displays necessary to simulate ships, helicopters and other "Navy gear." The discovery of the transistor, followed by miniature electronic components resulted in the cancellation of the Trainer project.

However, Computing Devices did not stay dormant. The company opened a parallel line to design and produce aircraft instruments. The Horizontal Display Situation System used in NATO bombers was designed, and two prototype systems were built by Mr. A. Świderski. Unfortunately for Computing Devices, the production of this system was awarded to the rival company Breguet Co., in France.

The usefulness of the Air Navigation and Tactical Control System (ANTAC) developed for the Royal Canadian Air Force (RCAF) for the Argus maritime reconnaissance aircraft was proven over 15 years of operation. The purpose of ANTAC was to detect, locate and destroy enemy submarines. Several more types of instruments and systems were designed and built over the years by Computing Devices for the armies, navies and air forces of Canada and other countries.

Dr. G. Gliński left the company in the 1960s to teach full time at the University of Ottawa, and Norton-Spychalski retired in the 1970s. Computing Devices, however, is still operating at full force, although now as a division of the U.S.-based General Dynamics. Sometimes Computing Devices is even called the grandfather of Northern Silicon Valley.

Minister C.D. Howe's decision to bring Polish engineers and other specialists to Canada to help with the war effort proved to be a good idea for both sides. Well-educated and experienced Polish specialists eased the difficulties Canada had in supplying adequate personnel for the wartime industries, and the Poles could work in their chosen professions, contributing meaningfully to the struggle of the free world with the Nazi dictatorship. When the war ended, the temporary arrangement was so advantageous to Canada, and to the Polish specialists, that it was made permanent, and they were given permission to stay in the country as its citizens. They have earned this right by their work, their expertise and their attachment to the new land.

CHAPTER FIVE

ŻURA AND FRIENDS

The end of World War II signalled the closing of many factories, including most of those active in the aviation field. Fortunately for Polish aeronautical engineers, the Canadian government decided that Canada should have an aircraft industry and should design a modern passenger airplane powered by English engines and a fighter plane powered by an engine designed and manufactured in Canada. Two new companies replaced the wartime factories: A.V. Roe Ltd. replaced the Victory Aircraft, and The Orenda Ltd. was organized to design and build the engines for a new fighter-bomber. Almost all enthusiasts of the legendary Avro Arrow have heard the name of Janusz Żurakowski—the test pilot who flew the plane.

Janusz ("Żura") Żurakowski was born in Ryżawka in eastern Poland when World War I was just beginning, in September 1914. His older brother Bronisław grew up to be a pilot and aircraft designer. Evidently, the family had an aviation bug. Janusz first flew a plane at the tender age of 15. In 1937 he was already a fully qualified pilot and a graduate of a well-known military air academy in Dęblin. Two years later he fought the Nazi invaders in the September Campaign in unequal air duels under Polish skies.

"I took off from our airport in a PZL P-7," recalled Żurakowski, "and, as I gathered speed, I noticed a formation of seven Dornier 17 planes over Dęblin. On my approach, they opened fire."

> I couldn't get close enough to shoot since the German planes were so much faster; but when the pilots saw that I was keeping back, they slowed down and opened fire on me again. At that time, I started firing as well, but after a few seconds my machine guns jammed. With some satisfaction, however, I saw a bright streak of steam issuing from one of the planes—a sign of a shot-out fuel tank. When I opened fire again, the German planes began to distance themselves very quickly. This game repeated itself a few times. The Germans were hoping that they would shoot me, and I was counting on the plane that was hit slowing down. The Germans gave up first. They sped off and eventually vanished on the horizon. When I returned to Ułęż, we found several holes in the wings of my aircraft.

When the campaign ended, Żurakowski managed to escape to Great Britain where he joined the Royal Air Force. In 1942, Janusz, whose unpronounceable last name was abbreviated to "Żura," was named commander of a fighter squadron 316, and in the next year he was promoted to captain and named a deputy commander of the fighter wing based in the famous base at Norholt. For his achievements in the Battle of Britain, he received numerous decorations, including the highest Polish decoration for valour, the Virtuti Militari Cross.

At the end of the war, Żura was transferred to the Imperial Test Pilots School in Boscombe Down and flew most of the new British and American planes. He not only flew them, but he also designed two new figures of aerial acrobatic manoeuvres that were regarded as impossible to execute. Żura proved them doable. In all, he test-flew over 100 new aerial constructions, and as an aside, set a new flight speed record from London to Copenhagen and back. The attempt was organized by Gloster to sell the Meteor IV to the Danish Air Force, and it succeeded. Acknowledged as one of the best acrobatic pilots in the UK, Żura gave a spectacular display at the 1951 Farnborough Airshow.

Also at Farnborough, Żura demonstrated a new aerobatics manoeuvre, the "Zurabatic Cartwheel." James Hamilton-Peeterson (cited in Wikipedia) described this complicated aerial figure as follows:

> ...he suspended the Gloster Meteor G-7-1 prototype he was flying, in a vertical cartwheel.... The cartwheel used the dangerously asymmetric behaviour the Meteor had with one engine throttled back. The manoeuvre started with a vertical climb to 4000 ft [1.2 kilometres] by which point the aircraft had slowed to only 80 mph [128 kilometres per hour]. Cutting the power of one engine caused the Meteor to pivot. When the nose was pointing downwards, the second engine was throttled back and the aircraft continued to rotate

through a further 360 degrees on momentum alone having lost nearly all vertical velocity. Carrying out the cartwheel and recovering from it with entering an inverted spin (which the Meteor could not be brought out of) required great skill.

The important thing, however, was that the stunt was actually quite safe for the machine and for the pilot. There was no element of cavalier risk in what Żurakowski demonstrated. Before attempting the aerobatic figure, he had spent hours calculating all possible elements of the manoeuvre using a slide rule.

In 1952, Żurakowski obtained employment in Canada, engaged to test flight the new fighter CF-100 "Canuck," one of the best and most modern fighter planes of the 1950s.

"I sent a letter to the firm, A.V. Roe Canada," Żurakowski recalled in a conversation with Marek Kusiba, "which belonged to the same parent company as Gloster (Hawker Siddeley Group), and shortly after, I received a positive reply to my request. I was to come to Canada as quickly as possible, since the CF-100s, which the firm was beginning to put into production, were awaiting crucial tests."

Żurakowski mentioned in the interview that his wife Anna supported him in his decision to immigrate to Canada. Apparently, she was feeling uncomfortable in England, where they were considered "foreign," and wanted to leave Europe for good.

In England, when I told my friends at Gloster about my intended departure, one of my colleagues shouted, "You've got to be kidding! Canada's such a primitive country, especially when it comes to the aviation industry!" My Canadian-born boss, on the other hand, stated quite firmly, "Nothing of the sort. There is no difference between Canada and England." After my arrival, I quickly came to terms with the fact that neither statement was true: Canada was not a primitive country, but neither was it just like England.

How was the experienced test pilot, a war hero and one of those, to whom (according to Winston Churchill) "so many owed so much to so few" received in Canada? Under the headline "Inventor of Zurabatic Cartwheel joins AVRO as test pilot," the *Toronto Telegram* published this comment: "Zurakowski—he is small and balding and looks anything but a test pilot."

Żurakowski, however, was a born test pilot. While still working on CF-100, he was informed that the maximum speed in level flight was 87 percent of the speed of sound. Żurakowski asked what would happen if the pilot was to exceed this speed, for example, in a dive. He was told that was the maximum speed in the instruction manual and that wind-tunnel tests showed that at 90 percent of the speed of sound, the pilot lost control of the plane.

For Żurakowski it was obvious that an accidental excess of speed could occur in flight, so the plane should be tested to investigate its characteristics and to supplement the manual with instructions for the pilot if he should lose control over the machine as a result of excess speed. So Żurakowski made repeated flights, increasing the maximum speed in a dive, until finally reaching the speed of sound. The sonic boom was heard throughout the entire district and caused a great sensation. It was the first time that a plane with straight

Janusz Żurakowski preparing for a test flight of the legendary Avro Arrow

wings had broken the sound barrier without the help of a rocket engine. And it happened in a Canadian-made plane flown by a Polish test pilot!

In March 1958, Żura flew the legendary prototype construction, a CF-105 Avro Arrow fighter interceptor being designed in Toronto. The 32-ton jet was airborne for 35 minutes at a height of 1.5 kilometres and a speed of 250 knots. Żura stated:

> On March 25, 1958, when I completed my first flight in the Avro Arrow, I hoped that for many years Canada would have a very modern and very good defense aircraft. This was the belief shared not only by the team of specialists at A.V. Roe, but also by the Canadian people. Yes, Canadians wanted to be proud of this new aircraft produced in Canada.

The first flight test conducted in 1958 confirmed that the hope was not an impossible dream. The Arrow performed splendidly, and the prognosis for its future was excellent. Żura made over 20 test flights of the plane and reached a speed of Mach 1.89 in it. In November 1958, "Spud" Potocki, flying the Arrow with American Pratt & Whitney engines, which were less powerful than Canadian Iroquois engines, reached a speed of Mach 1.96—close to twice the speed of sound. This information, however, was not released before the cancellation of the project.

On September 24, 1958, the Toronto newspaper *The Telegram* quoted a statement by former Chief of General Staff Lieutenant General Guy Simmons. General Simmons said that he had criticized from the beginning any plan to spend large sums of money on "The last of the fighters." He said the Arrow was just that: "The last of its line and kind."

"This statement," said Żurakowski in his 1998 speech at a gala organized by the Canadian Heritage Aerospace Foundation on the anniversary of the maiden flight of the Arrow, "reminds me of the situation 65 years ago when I trained in Poland as a fighter pilot. Lots of 'experts' were trying to convince me fighter aircraft had no future because new bombers were faster than our fighter aircraft. I was stubborn and stayed with fighters. Thank God. England in 1940 had good fighters. They won the Battle of Britain, preventing a German invasion and probably world domination by Hitler."

In February 1959, the dream of building and test flying a new, ultra-modern fighter plane ended. Avro Arrow was no more, and there was little of interest left in the air for Janusz Żurakowski:

Employees of the Avro plant in Malton cheering Janusz Żurakowski after a successful flight of the Avro Arrow

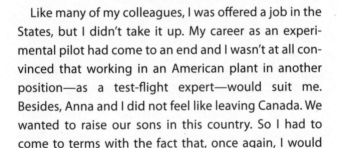

Like many of my colleagues, I was offered a job in the States, but I didn't take it up. My career as an experimental pilot had come to an end and I wasn't at all convinced that working in an American plant in another position—as a test-flight expert—would suit me. Besides, Anna and I did not feel like leaving Canada. We wanted to raise our sons in this country. So I had to come to terms with the fact that, once again, I would have to start my life from scrap...I mean, from scratch.

And in summing up his feelings regarding the cancellation of the project, Żura said, "Governments and torches can destroy an aircraft but they cannot destroy hope and aspiration, and the majesty of the questing spirit. In the hearts of the people the dream lives on."

Such a brief and dry encyclopedic note does not do justice to one of the most interesting men who came from Poland to Canada, to help create the new country. Test pilots are a separate breed of flyers. Their work is to try out in flight, risking their lives, the theoretical constructions of aircraft designers. Their work is to test the design so that others may fly it safely. It would seem that test pilots have a death wish and are ready for an accident daily.

Nothing is further from the truth—at least, as far as Żurakowski was concerned. There was almost no element of risk in his work because he did all he could to minimize the risk. Before he tried anything in the air, he spent long hours analyzing the design and the task the plane was to perform. He used his vast knowledge of aircraft design and his extensive practical experience in the field. His method was to find out as many characteristics of the new plane as possible before he attempted to take it in the air and run the machine through its paces and to verify that his estimates and suspicions were correct.

Janusz Żurakowski tested the first Avro Arrow in March 1958. The flight from Malton airport was historic for Canadian aircraft industry. Żurakowski was piloting an aircraft that was doubtlessly at that time the best, the most modern supersonic fighter interceptor in the world. It was the biggest and the heaviest fighter of its time, but it was also equipped with the best electronics, navigational equipment and armament control. In his expert opinion, the fighter flew well. When the maiden flight was over, Żurakowski was greeted on the tarmac with an enthusiastic welcome of 10,000 employees of Avro.

Further work on the design, however, was absolutely necessary. According to the Department of National Defence specifications, CF-105 was supposed to reach the speed of Mach 2—twice the speed of sound. The first machines could not do that: their British-constructed Pratt and Whitney engines were not powerful enough. The first five fighters produced at Malton had to be rebuilt. The sixth one, however, was almost finished, and it was equipped with the more powerful Orenda Iroquois engines. It would seem that the specifications would be met. Unofficially, they were—it is rumoured that Żurakowski's friend and comrade in arms, Władysław "Spud" Jaworski, took "The Arrow" to over Mach 2, but that was never officially confirmed. The truth, as with many other aspects of the Avro Arrow story, will never be known.

Janusz Żurakowski's career ended practically with "The Arrow." He received the McKee Trophy in 1958, the highest honour for a Canadian flyer. The trophy is awarded by the Canadian Aeronautics and Space Institute to a Canadian citizen who has made an outstanding, contemporary achievement in aerospace operations. The award was founded in 1927 by James Dalzell McKee and is the oldest aviation award in Canada.

Żura was inducted into the Canadian Aviation Hall of Fame. The citation reads: "The dedication of his aeronautical skills to the successful flight testing of Canada's first supersonic aircraft resulted in outstanding benefit to Canadian aviation." His skills and devotion to his work were recognized and appreciated. On July 23, 1999, CFB Cold Lake (Alberta) Aerospace Engineering Test Establishment named its new facility the Żurakowski Building, and in September 2000, he became an Honorary Fellow of the Society of

Experimental Test Pilots, joining the ranks of Charles Lindbergh, Neil Armstrong and Igor Sikorsky.

Żurakowski, however, was heartbroken over the decision to end the work on the CF-105 Avro Arrow. The rest of his long and fruitful life was spent in the Kaszuby region of Ontario, in the Kartuzy Lodge he built for those seeking rest and recreation. In 2003, his adopted hometown built Żurakowski Park, in recognition of his contributions to the community as well as to the world. Two statues, one of Janusz Żurakowski and the other of his beloved Avro Arrow, stand in the arrow-shaped park (an elongated triangle that reminds the observer of the Avro Arrow's profile) at the crossroads of two main streets in Barry's Bay, Ontario. And the former Gloster Aircraft company airfield at Hucclecote in England has become a residential division in Gloucester and features Zura Avenue.

Żurakowski Park in Barry's Bay, Ontario

Janusz Żurakowski was the best known and the most honoured Polish flier in Canada, but he was not the only one. I have already mentioned Żurakowski's colleague on the Avro Arrow project, Władysław "Spud" Jaworski. In later years, Jaworski taught American astronauts how to fly the lunar module. Neil Armstrong owes him a debt in making the famous small step onto the surface of the moon.

Another of the Polish defenders of Britain in its air battle with the Nazi air force, Jan Borowczyk, came to Canada in 1952, but he was not destined to help with the legendary project at Malton. Even though he had also demonstrated his flying prowess by flying in the Polish fighter squadron 315, he ended up at Canadian Westinghouse Co. in Hamilton as manufacturing methods manager for steam-generating equipment, pumps and turbines.

From 1960 until his retirement in 1984, Borowczyk worked for the Canadian civil service in Ottawa as a systems engineer for Canada Post. He planned the design and operations of major postal terminals in Ottawa, Calgary and Victoria, and made improvements in the operational systems in Montréal, Halifax, Vancouver and Winnipeg.

Another fighter ace from the war period, former commander of the legendary Polish squadron 303 and one of the most effective Allied squadrons during the Battle of Britain, Tadeusz Kotz, came to Collingwood, Ontario, in 1956, engaged by the Martin Baker company. He started as a designer of ejector seats for the Avro Arrow, but the cancellation of the program ended his career in aviation. Kotz had to take up any job offered and ended up drafting blueprints for the construction of refrigerators.

When the Canadian Aviation Hall of Fame included Janusz Żurakowski, his name was not the only Polish name added to the list. In the same year, another Polish Canadian, son of Polish immigrants to Canada, was awarded this honour: Andrew Mynarski, a recipient of the highest decoration for valour, the Victoria Cross.

Andrew Mynarski was born in Winnipeg in 1916, enlisting in the Winnipeg Rifles in 1940. A year later he transferred to the RCAF, trained as an air gunner and joined the 419 squadron, where he completed 12 operational flights. On June 12, 1944, Mynarski and the crew aboard a Lancaster bomber were sent to attack a target at Cambrai in France. The aircraft came under heavy attack, and both engines failed. As the plane lost altitude, the crew bailed out while Mynarski tried to save the rear gunner trapped in the turret.

Mynarski's attempts were unsuccessful, and he finally jumped from the flaming aircraft but not without a final salute to his comrade. Mynarski was found with his clothes and parachute still aflame, and he later died from his injuries. The rear gunner miraculously survived the crash and explained that if Mynarski had not stayed behind, the gunner most certainly would have died. Mynarski's heroism earned him the Victoria Cross.

Finally, although this is not a complete list of the achievements of Polish pilots under Canadian skies, one more name deserves mention. Michał Zubko came to Canada much later and was not a veteran of

World War II, yet he did deserve to be inducted in the Canadian Aviation Hall of Fame. The citation reads:

> His vision of the needs of the people in a large, remote and challenging area of Canada, along with his persistence, ability, courage and dedication to carry out his dream contributed immensely to the betterment of life at isolated communities in the Mackenzie Delta, and resulted in the advancement of aviation in Canada.

Michał Zubko dedicated himself to serving the North, providing the first commercial air service north of the Arctic Circle. His charter service vastly improved the lives of people living along the Mackenzie Delta and along the Arctic coast, providing a vital link between these isolated communities and the world. In 1995 his contribution to the North was recognized when the Mike Zubko Airport at Inuvik was named in his honour.

It may safely be said that Polish fliers made their mark in Canada.

CHAPTER SIX

THE POLES ARE COMING

According to Statistics Canada, in 1931 about 145,000 people in Canada declared Polish nationality; they comprised 1.4 percent of the country's total population. By 1941 the number of Poles in Canada exceeded 167,000; by 1951, Canada was home to almost 220,000 Poles. The latest data, according to Statistics Canada (2006 census), lists the number of Canadians of Polish descent at 984,565.

When World War II ended, thousands of Polish officers and soldiers were left without a homeland to go back to. For political reasons, the Allies gave Poland over to the Communist Soviet Union, and Poles knew very well what that meant. They had no illusions. The members of the armed forces that fought the Nazis the longest, from September 1, 1939, were bureaucratically transformed into DPs—"displaced persons."

It is important to understand the situation of Polish veterans and their mindset at the time. The end of World War II in Europe found the Polish Armed Forces in the West (usually referred to by their Polish-language acronym PSZnZ) located in several countries of Western Europe. The armed forces numbered about 250,000 officers and soldiers, mainly army, with the important addition of the air force and naval personnel. Even though the European continent was in those years full of soldiers in various uniforms, the PSZnZ was a sizeable force in that context. The Forces were a well-managed army with battle experience in all the-atres of war, proven under fire and well equipped in modern arms and military vehicles. They fought the Germans from Norway through Battle of Britain, the Atlantic and Arctic convoys, Northern Africa, Italy, France, Holland to the final line of attack in May 1945.

When the guns were finally silenced, the PSZnZ was the strongest military force left without a country to disperse to. Politically, they believed the war had ended only provisionally. After all, in September 1939, Poland was attacked by two powers—Nazi Germany and Soviet Russia. Germany was defeated, but the other attacker had become an ally and was rewarded the ultimate prize—the territory of the country where the whole conflict started. Persuaded by the English authorities, the Poles waited for the suppos-edly free elections in Soviet-occupied Poland. Most of them, with past experience in Polish-Russian relations, were sceptical, and were to be proven right by the 40 years of Cold War to follow.

The Polish Forces interpreted the results of the February 1945 Yalta Conference as a symbol of betrayal of Poland and Polish people by the Allies, who agreed to hand over the area inhabited by the Poles to the Soviets to rule as they wished. They saw the Yalta Conference results as creating Poland, occupied by the Nazi forces since September 1939, that the Soviet army was now to occupy. For five years the soldiers of the Polish Forces had fought, hoping to return to their free country. Now, the troops were in shock. They were aware of the situation but could not comprehend the motives for "the betrayal." Rumours circulating throughout the units indicated the ultimate distrust between the Poles and their British commanders. According to that false "news," the British provisionally deployed some Ghurka divisions around the quarters of the 3rd Karpaty Division, vets of the Monte Cassino battle, "to take care of the Poles in case of trouble."

The soldiers could see only a bleak future in the face of Soviet occupation of Poland. One of the Polish airmen reflected on the news of the Yalta Conference: "I wonder if it is all worth anything. If the Germans get me now, I will not even know if I die for Poland, for England or for Russia."

They were not alone in their assessment of the terms agreed to in Yalta. An American politician, Representative D.J. Flood considered the Yalta Conference to be a disaster comparable only to the Pearl Harbor catastrophe.

On May 22, 1946, British Foreign Secretary in the Labour government replacing Sir Winston Churchill's wartime cabinet, Ernest Bevin, stood up in the Parliament and declared that the Polish Forces were being demilitarized and disbanded. A quarter of a million veterans and their families were left almost exclusively to their own devices in a strange land. They held no hope of returning to their homeland, for which they fought for over five long years. The only help devised by the British government was the organization of Polish Resettlement Corps, to assist the veterans in their efforts of finding a new home in the world within a proscribed time limit of two years.

British authorities dreamed of transferring the entire army back to Poland, under the Communist regime. The Provisional Government led by the Communists was, of course, ready to comply and accept the forces on its own terms—without their experienced command, and preferably disarmed. Some soldiers, though few, were taken in by the Communist propaganda. Some could not see another way out and longed to join their families left behind under the Communist rule. Most, however, remained without an idea what to do.

Officers were equally as lost as enlisted men. Some attempts at directing and advising were made, but it was far from systematic. However, the situation generated surprising improvised achievements, as for instance the activity of second lieutenant Leonard Ramczykowski.

In 1931, Ramczykowski graduated from University of Poznań in Poland with degrees in Polish and German literature. He was a dedicated teacher, but the war interrupted his pedagogical career. He was drafted in September 1939, and after the September Campaign, served in the underground army of the Polish resistance movement. In 1940, he was arrested by the infamous Soviet secret police NKVD, spent 10 months in the Wilno jail and was sentenced to five years of hard labour in a Siberian work camp in Workuta. In 1942 he was allowed to leave Soviet Russia as a soldier of the II Corps. In that unit he served through the Italian Campaign fighting the Germans at Monte Cassino, Ancona and Bologna.

Delegated to the administration of adaptation courses, he again picked up his teaching career, as he tried to prepare his fellow soldiers for civilian life. It is rumoured that while still in service, he used his military equipment to teach geography and local history to his comrades in arms. Years later, his pupils wrote about him upon his demise:

> He was a passionate teacher. While we were moving up the Italian boot, he explained to us the local history from Roman times onwards. I can still remember the lecture he gave us at Trasimeno Lake, indicating the locale of the events through the military field glasses. Without books, without a blackboard, he still taught us rudimentary Latin, Polish and classical history. It gave me courage for further studies later on.

In 1952, Ramczykowski managed to get permission to immigrate to Canada. His first job was teaching at a First Nations school in the Thunder Bay area. Ojibwa chiefs appreciated his assistance over the many years of work with First Nations youth. He was named an honorary Ojibwa chief and was given the Native name Niganate, meaning "leading light." A symbolic name, equally proper for a man who helped the Ojibwa, and the comrade in arms, who did his best to help his fellow soldiers adapt to civilian life after a devastating conflict.

Canada agreed to accept some of the displaced veterans, but Canadian authorities were at the same time afraid of the future the country faced. Remembering well the years following World War I and the economic depression of the 1920s, Ottawa restricted immigration following World War II, to preserve jobs for their own citizens and the veterans returning home from the trenches. Thus, the Canadian government agreed to accept roughly 4000 Polish veterans seeking a new homeland. It was not by accident that this was precisely the number of German prisoners of war returning from Canada to Germany after the cessation of hostilities. Polish officers and men would replace on Canadian farms the workers from the army they had helped to defeat.

Most of the Polish vets came to Canada on two-year contracts as agricultural workers. The veterans were often well-educated, experienced professional soldiers, with five years of brutal campaign behind them and well travelled over the world. They were sent to remote Canadian farms as hired hands to help Canadian farmers with little education and often a limited knowledge of the world. The contrast was dramatic.

Some of their memoirs, published in later years, describe comic or tragicomic conflicts; they resound with bitterness toward the Canadian authorities that did not seem to appreciate the irony of their situation. For example, there was the case of a Polish officer, fresh from a German prisoner of war camp, who was directed as a farmhand to a Canadian farmer of

Polish soldiers arrive en route to farms in Canada, 1946

German descent. It took Canadian Red Cross intervention to resolve the conflict.

The post–World War II wave of Polish immigrants
to Canada was drastically different from the pre-war
pioneers. They came from all walks of society, and
about 20 percent were highly qualified professionals.
Some spoke fluent English or French; some came with
sizeable savings. Their beginnings were difficult,
though definitely easier than the start of the life in
Canada experienced by the immigrants of the first half
of the 20th century. At the same time, the contribution they made to Canada was incomparably greater.
After all, Toronto subway trains still have tunnels
to run in, designed by a Polish immigrant, the CN
Tower still stands on foundations prepared by Peter

Brzozowicz, and countless other less visible traces document Polish contribution to the great Canadian success story of the 20th century.

Władysław Henoch was born in 1913 in a small town of Krzeszowice near Cracow, the son of Dr. Józef Henoch, a lawyer and an administrator of the estates of Countess Potocka, the descendant of one of the great noble families of Poland. The family prospered and educated their children well. Władysław graduated from Jagiellonian University in Cracow (the fifth-oldest university in the world) with degrees in geography and geology. In 1938 he left Poland to take part in a round-the-world expedition of the Polish Scouts yacht *Poleszuk*. Little did he expect that it would take over 30 years before he would be able to see his native land once more.

The sailing expedition was already underway, and Henoch joined it in the Senegalese port of Conakry. The *Poleszuk* sailed to British Guyana, where the exotic Polish flag raised the eyebrows of the local authorities, and the equipment of the sailing vessel received undisguised admiration. From there, through Grenada, Barbados, Martinique and the Dominican Republic and Havana, the yacht reached Miami and New York. By the time the emotional welcome from Americans of Polish origins was over, it was September 1, 1939. Poland was at war with Nazi Germany, and, two weeks later, with Soviet Russia. The around-the-world sailing expedition was over.

Henoch sailed back to Europe on a passenger liner to join the Polish Army in France. Reporting to the Polish Army recruiting centre in Paris, Henoch was assigned to the Warsaw Regiment of Light Artillery being formed in Brittany. With the unit, he fought a brief war on the famous Maginot Line, and, with the regiment acting as a component of the French 8th Army, fought the German forces until the capitulation of France.

Being well aware of what the Germans had been doing in Poland from September 1939 onwards, the command of the division decided to leave France and take refuge in Switzerland. In his memoirs published decades later in Canada, Henoch wrote:

> I had not come to join the Polish Army from the United States to spend the rest of the war in the safety of internment in Switzerland.... I therefore reported to the C.O. of the Regiment before we came under Swiss jurisdiction telling him that I refused to be interned and that I hoped to make my way through German occupied territory to the south of France.... Lieutenant Henryk S. Kożuchowski was willing to join me and we were given permission to proceed.

On their way through southern France, the two men were captured by a German unit but escaped and continued through Spain to reach Lisbon in Portugal. From there, they sailed to England to join the Polish army once again. Kożuchowski died in Poland in 1944 while working as an agent for British intelligence.

Wartime service took Henoch to Scotland, where he prepared coastal defences in case of a German invasion, and where he met his future wife. Before the wedding ceremony could be concluded, Henoch was reassigned from Scotland to Northern Africa, to fight the German units at Tobruk.

Henoch ended up in Palestine and Iraq. In October 1943, his unit, the famous Carpathian Brigade, was transferred to Italy to take part in a legendary (for the Poles) battle at Monte Cassino. The Americans, the British and the New Zealanders failed; the Carpathian Brigade took the fortress and opened the road to Rome for the Allied armies. Wounded at Monte Cassino, Lieutenant Henoch continued to serve, and after the battle for Ancona, he was decorated with the Virtuti Militari Cross, the highest Polish decoration for valour in armed service and equivalent to the Victoria Cross.

From Italy, Henoch was sent back to England to once again take up his university-acquired profession of geographer and to work with the ministry of information, a department of the Polish Government in Exile. That did not last long. In February 1946, the new British government rescinded the recognition of the Polish Government in Exile and disbanded its departments. Thousands of Poles, who had fought the Nazis since September 1, 1939, were left to their own devices. Henoch with his wife and children decided to sail to Canada and buy a farm there. (Their wedding had finally taken place in Edinburgh on April 3, 1945.)

For no particular reason, the Henochs chose a farm near Welland, Ontario. Farming proved too difficult for the geographer and officer, so Henoch got a job with Atlas Steel. After about three years, the family, comprising by that time of parents, six children and mother-in-law, gave up on farming altogether, and Henoch applied for a job in Ottawa, trying to return once more to his profession. He was accepted for a position in the Geographical Branch of the

Ministry of Mines and Technical Surveys. At 43, the sailor, a decorated veteran of French and Italian campaigns, a former farmer and a miller was to embark on a completely new career.

That, however, proved to be the last episode in the rich life of Władysław Henoch. He stayed in his field of expertise until retirement, devoting his interest to surveys and exploration of glaciers. His work took him to King Edward Island in the Canadian Arctic, to the delta of the Mackenzie River and the Yukon coast. His last professional achievement involved studying and mapping glaciers in the Canadian Rockies. His name is found on the map of Peyto Glacier, the first modern glacier map done in Canada following the French and Swiss map publishing practices.

In 1997, W.E.S. Henoch published his memoirs in Toronto under the title *One Man Many Lives*. He ended the text with these words: "I am a Pole who remains proud of his Polish heritage. I have put down roots in my new country and I am now a proud Canadian."

Henoch's story and his contribution to the post-war development of Canada was only one of a long series. The Canadian armaments industry and other sectors developed during the war years placed Canada in the forefront of modern industrial economies of the world. Polish engineers who helped build the industry during this time contributed greatly to the success of industrial Canada in the second half of the 20th century.

Stanisław Orłowski's part in the war began when the Russians transported him, along with thousands of his countrymen, to a labour camp in Siberia. He escaped, and through the Middle East he joined the Polish

armed forces, to fight in the Italian campaign. Demobilized in 1945, he studied economics and architecture
at the Leicester University. There, he met his future
wife Krystyna, who also contributed to the war effort
by joining the Women's Auxiliary Air Force (WAAF).

Orłowski graduated from the Leicester University in
1951 and began working for a local architectural firm.
He did not feel safe, however, in the atmosphere of the
Cold War in Europe. There was always the danger of
another upheaval, and the Orłowskis had had enough
of war. Thus, in 1952, the couple decided to move to
Canada. They chose this country because it was safer
and was farther from the potential area of conflict, but
also because Canada was closer to Europe in lifestyle
and culture than the U.S. or Australia.

Orłowski benefited from the earlier achievements of
his colleagues, who had arrived and started working in
Canada during World War II. He found a job in his
profession on his second day in Toronto, by joining
the Ontario Department of Public Works. Being
a rather restless person, at least professionally, he left
public service for a position with Page and Steel, but
a few years later returned to government employment
at the federal level. He gained the position of area
architect, and later as acting district architect working
for a planning office for Ontario. He designed hospitals, post offices and housing for Native people and the
RCMP. The years 1957 to 1965 were a construction
boom period in Toronto and Ontario's history, and
Stanisław Orłowski contributed greatly to the shape
this boom took.

In 1965 he once more left the government to return
to private architectural practice with the firm of

Allward and Gouinlock. He was instrumental in the design of the Queen Elizabeth Hospital in Toronto as well as numerous schools—particularly when he once again joined the public service by winning the competition for the position of Chief Research Assistant of School Planning, and later Chief Research Architect. The last advancement was a decision made personally by then minister of education, and later the premier of Ontario, William Davis, who was impressed with Orłowski's work.

In a conversation with Polish historian and biographer Aleksandra Ziółkowska, Orłowski stated that the years 1967 to 1974 were the most fruitful and the best in his professional life. He designed 22 colleges, and the Research Institute published 35 studies under his tenure and organized 14 conferences on school planning and four on university and college planning, inviting experts from all over the world. Orłowski also received invitations to lecture in the United States and Europe.

More than 250 buildings in Ontario were designed by or with Stanisław Orłowski's input. He worked at over 40 sites, and his name is synonymous with school planning expertise in many countries all over the world. Orłowski is a member of the College of Fellows of the Royal Canadian Institute of Architects, an honour bestowed on architects who have made an exceptional contribution to their profession.

Orłowski finished his career as Chief Architect for the Ministry of Colleges and Universities, Ontario, and was a powerful presence in the Polish World Scouting movement and the Polish Canadian Congress. Krystyna's support took the tangible form of editing every paper Stan wrote and assisting him in every presentation. They were married for 54 years and lived to see a free and democratic Poland and their adopted homeland Canada grow to the status of one of the leading industrial nations of the world.

As mentioned in an earlier chapter, Polish engineers made their mark on Canadian soil during World War II. Their work and achievements cleared the path for their professional colleagues in later years. One of the more prominent immigrants in this profession was Ludwik Alejski, born in Poznań in 1921. Conscripted into the army, he fought in the September Campaign of 1939. In 1940 he was arrested by the Nazi Gestapo and spent five years in the infamous concentration camp at Mauthausen. Freed by the Allies, he enlisted in the II Corps for the Italian campaign. Demobilized in England, he studied at the University of London, graduating in 1954 with a degree in structural engineering.

Ludwik Alejski came to Canada in 1958 and settled in Toronto. He joined the consulting engineer company Carruthers and Wallace Ltd., eventually becoming its vice-president. In the course of his professional career, he designed such spectacular structures as the Toronto Dominion Bank Pavilion, Eaton Centre, Bell Canada Exchange Building, Confederation of Life building, Robarts Library at the University of Toronto, Roy Thomson Hall and the Encyclopaedia Britannica building. For the design of the Toronto Dominion Bank Pavilion in 1969 and of the Robarts Library in 1974, he received Canadian Consulting Engineering awards. In 1986 he was awarded the Engineering Medal of Excellence.

Les Bachorz also survived the war with the Nazis, although he was too young to enlist and participate in the September Campaign. He was not too young, however, to take an active part in the resistance movement, cross the border in flight from the Gestapo and be arrested and deported by the Soviet secret police NKVD. Like many of his countrymen, he took advantage of the Sikorski-Majski Agreement of 1941 and left the Soviet Union in the ranks of the Polish Corps led by General Władysław Anders. This allowed him to reach England and join the RAF.

After the war, Bachorz took up university studies first at Cardiff, then in London, coming to Canada in 1952 following his many colleagues, who were Polish engineers. Since 1956, his company, L.C. Bachorz Associates, executed over 650 projects in Canada, the United States and in the Bahamas. Bachorz was a member of the Engineering Institute of Canada, was the president of the Association of Polish Engineers and one of the initiators of the Canada Poland Chamber of Commerce.

Other Poles, with less education and lower qualifications, contributed to Canada's creation in different ways. In 1984, Julia Jarosińska published her memoirs included in a fascinating collection of first-hand accounts published under a Polish language title that translates as *The Disappointed, The Disillusioned, The Content*. I feel her story could not be told better by anyone else. Thus, I've translated some fragments of her memoirs:

"My road to Canada was long and led through faraway lands. It led through Asia and Africa, and lasted over seventeen years," said Jarosińska.

Julia's family, as well as the family of her future husband, Sławek, lived in the Nowogródek region of eastern Poland. When Soviet Russia invaded Poland on September 17, 1939, they found themselves under Soviet occupation and were forcibly transported east, to Kazakhstan. They regained their freedom in August 1942, when the Soviet authorities allowed some Polish people to leave the Soviet territory together with the army units formed under the command of General Władysław Anders. Julia and her mother were sent by the British authorities to Eastern Africa, while Sławek continued with the army units through Persia, India, Palestine to Italy and finally, when the war ended in 1945, to Britain.

> In 1956 I received a letter from Sławek, who at that time was already in Canada. He got my address from our mutual friends residing in Argentina. He wanted me to come to Canada to share his life.... I accepted, but the administrative progress was impeded by my British passport issued in Dar es Salaam. Canada was at that time distrustful of African British.... Finally, on September 22, 1957, I was ready to travel to the other side of the world.... My passport was stamped with a visa listing my profession as "fiancée." If I did not marry, I was allowed to stay in Canada till January 1, 1958..... After 34 hours of travel I arrived in Vancouver.... My first impressions were very positive. In England, I had to wear a coat; here it was sunny and warm.... In the evening, Sławek took me to the Polish St. Casimir church. Two days later we were married.

Ocean Falls was a surprise to Julia, who had spent the last 15 years in Africa. It was a small town, found on few maps, with no direct road connection to the outside world. The town was visited twice a week by a company supply ship and occasionally (if the weather was nice) by hydroplanes. In 1957, Ocean Falls was blooming. The paper and pulp plant ran 24/7 and employed about 1000 workers. Finding housing for all the workers and their families in a limited area became a problem, so a new subdivision was built in neighbouring Martin Valley, accessible only on a twisting road almost three kilometres away, along the coast of the bay. Martin Valley was the subdivision of private residences, while all other buildings belonged to Crown Zellerbach Ltd. and were rented from the company. If you wanted to buy a house, you had to wait your turn, which sometimes took a few years.

The young immigrant couple had to work for everything from scratch. Gradually, Julia got to know other Polish people in the town, most of them wartime immigrants—vets of the II Corps, DPs transported during the war to Germany as workers or survivors of Soviet population movements. There were also some who came to Canada before the war. She was astonished at the speed with which they had assimilated. Almost every one mixed Polish and English words and spoke to their children in English. This American-style assimilation did not appeal to Jarosińska. As she stated in her memoirs, she would not dream of using English to speak to a countryman, least of all to her own children. This was the time before multiculturalism became an official Canadian policy, and even teachers advised parents to speak to their children in English, unaware that this attitude harmed children by destroying their connection with the language and culture of their forefathers.

"On August 31, 1958, our first daughter Irena was born," Julia continues her story. "Next year in December we welcomed a son named Kazimierz. I could at last practically experiment with my theories of bringing up children in the national Polish tradition in a new country....I took it as my duty to read to my children every single day."

Contrary to the education theories of the time, the Jarosiński children had no serious problems in school despite their parents insisting that they speak Polish at home. In 1966, other Polish parents asked Julia to teach Polish to their children. There were no heritage language programs in Canadian education at the time, so the lessons were conducted in Julia's kitchen. The lessons lasted throughout the summer, and the children enjoyed the additional education, but the process ended when school started again in September. It must be stated, however, that Julia's experiments with language education preceded present-day Canadian heritage language programs, established decades later with the help of another Polish Canadian, Jesse Flis, MP.

Julia states:

> I best remember an episode at some celebrations in the local Polish community. We were waiting for the program to start, and the children were busy talking. A lady neighbour commented: "One can see that they just arrived from Poland and they still have to speak Polish." She was astonished when I explained that my kids were all born in Canada and have never even visited Poland.

I visited Julia Jarosińska and her family in Lumby in 1986. They were still living in their little house, welcoming all the guests and serving excellent venison prepared "a la Polonaise." It was a unique experience to converse in Polish with Irka, their first-born daughter from Ocean Falls who now teaches in one of the schools on a First Nations reserve in British Columbia.

The Jarosiński family is not prominent in Canadian history, and their achievements may seem small scale and insignificant in the context of the whole country, but Julia's insistence on teaching Polish to her children and to those of her Polish Canadian neighbours underscores what was to become an official Canadian education policy and a dominant Canadian mindset differentiating Canada from other immigrant-welcoming nations, such as the United States. The Jarosiński children became Canadians, they participate in the life of this country, and they make their fortunes here. They also cultivate their Polish roots and travel to Poland where they have an opportunity to represent Canada as a truly free nation that allows its citizens to take advantage of the opportunity of material growth without demanding them to forsake their traditions.

CHAPTER SEVEN

POLES STANDING TALL

According to Statistics Canada, between 1951 and 1971, the community of Polish Canadians grew by almost half. There were almost 220,000 Canadians of Polish origin in 1951, and in 1971 the number grew to 315,000. The figures have to be treated with a grain of salt, however. Canadian census allows the respondent to determine his or her national origin, so there is no possibility of adjusting the figure to include people who described themselves as Canadian but who were of Polish origin. The Canadian ethnic mosaic of the second half of the 20th century comprised about 60 different ethnic groups; Poles were statistically in eighth or ninth place in this ranking. Most Polish Canadians lived in Ontario, although sizeable groups could still be found in major cities in other provinces, such as Montréal, Vancouver and Winnipeg.

Living in the cities influenced the professional characteristics of the group. Polish Canadians started, like
most immigrants, in predominantly farming communities, with fewer but equally important minor professional groups in mining. After World War II, Poles in
Canada moved to the cities, became part of the Canadian middle class and transferred their interest to
urban professions. A particularly high percentage of
new immigrants in the 1950s, '60s and '70s found
employment in higher education.

Unlike in the period immediately following the
war, the immigrants who came to Canada after 1955
were usually from Poland. Not all of them reached
Canadian shores because the Polish government of the
time discouraged emigration. Still, according to Canadian data, in the years 1955 to 1980, Canada welcomed over 60,000 immigrants from Poland. They
found employment in various walks of life, but a sur-
prisingly large number of them ended up at Canadian
universities.

Stefan Stykolt was born in 1923 in Zgierz in central
Poland. His family left the country at the beginning of
World War II, and after travelling to Romania, Italy,
Switzerland, France, Brazil and the U.S., they ended
up in Canada. Stefan's father, while in Poland, had
been a renowned scientist in the field of chemistry. He
established a furniture factory in Toronto, and Stefan
attended a prestigious Upper Canada College. In 1946
he graduated from Victoria College (presently part of
University of Toronto) with BA First Class Honours in
political science and economics.

He continued his studies at Harvard (where he
received a MA diploma) and in Cambridge. In 1951

he returned to Toronto to work for the literary, cultural and political journal *Canadian Forum*. From 1954 to 1959 he was the managing editor of the publication, and from 1955 to November 1957 was a member of a Royal Commission on Canada's Economic Prospects, initiated by Prime Minister Louis St. Laurent.

In 1958, Stefan Stykolt received his PhD from Harvard University; he began lecturing at the University of Toronto in 1955, and in 1961 he was named professor of political economics. His main field of interest was the history of Canadian economics, international cooperation and competition, tariffs and trade and monetary policies. One of the main proponents of free markets at that time, he authored numerous articles opposing state protectionism.

Stykolt is still considered one of the initiators of Canadian economic sciences. He was a popular lecturer and teacher, highly appreciated by his students for his sense of humour and for extensive knowledge outside the economic field (he spoke fluent French and adored the books of Marcel Proust). Unfortunately, cancer cut his life short at the young age of 39.

The *Canadian Journal of Economics and Political Science* published a farewell tribute to Stykolt under the title "The Living Name." His closest collaborator, Harry Johnson, wrote:

> Concentration on the pursuit of truth is the only self-justification, and scepticism the only form of self-defence and consolation, available to the intellectual in a country that knows itself to be a powerless pygmy

in a world of giants, and fears for its survival and its identity—whether it be Poland or Canada.

Stykolt's concepts and views were realized decades later within the so-called science of Reaganomics, and his prescription that the Canadian government needed to assert itself more in ensuring that Canadians ran the country's economy became the mantra of modern economics in Canada.

Another Polish immigrant to Canada who made a distinctive mark on the world stage was Zbigniew Brzeziński, a political scientist and statesman, and National Security Advisor to President Jimmy Carter. Brzeziński was born in Poland in 1928. His father Tadeusz Brzeziński was a professional diplomat, posted to Nazi Germany and Soviet Russia. In 1938, Tadeusz received a posting to Canada, where he and his family spent the war period.

Zbigniew Brzeziński entered McGill University in 1945, where he obtained his BA and MA degrees. He planned to further his studies in the United Kingdom before launching a diplomatic career in Canada, but his plans could not be realized as he was ruled ineligible for the scholarship he won, which was open only to British subjects. So he left for the United States and Harvard University, to continue a career that finally brought him to one of the most influential political appointments in the world.

Brzeziński remembered Canada and appreciated his years in Montréal. In an interview with Polish Canadian author Aleksandra Ziółkowska-Boehm, in her book *The Roots are Polish*, Brzeziński said:

My feeling of attachment towards Canada unfolded after the war ended. Before that, I was so engrossed in the war events that emotionally and intellectually I never left Poland. After 1945, I began to identify with Canada, appreciate the freedom, the marvellous opportunities she offered, the fundamental decency of the Canadian system and the Canadian people.

The Brzeziński family lived in Montréal, and as Brzeziński said in the interview, he at first did not take much interest in the affairs of the province. Only in the late 1940s did he come to identify more with the aspirations of Quebeckers and came to realize that they were in fact second-class citizens in their own country.

"I became very much a part of this country and did believe it would become my second home," he continued in the interview.

I have always harboured feelings of deep attachment to Canada, and I identified with her. Poland was the country of my childhood and of my historical and cultural roots. Canada, however, will remain forever the place of my adolescence, my coming of age, of my first adult friendships, my first romantic encounters, simply a place where I grew up. I value enormously all of these precious memories.... What I would say is that my Canadian experience, especially my secondary and post-secondary education helped me prepare to launch a successful career in the United States. It was precisely here, at McGill University, that I defined and developed my political interests and began studying the Soviet Union. It was where I found a new purpose in life.

Brzeziński's ambition was to enter the Canadian diplomatic service. He expressed his conviction that upon completing education in Britain, he would have returned to Canada and pursued his career here. Brzeziński, however, was not officially a Canadian citizen and that path to a diplomatic career was closed. So, he left for Harvard.

> If I had stayed in Canada, I might have become one of the few cabinet ministers who were not born in this country? In any case, there is no doubt that the process would have been much more challenging than in the United States where foreigners climbing up the ranks are not a rarity. In Canada, it does not happen too often, but, who knows, maybe I would have been a trail blazer.

Speaking of his own career, Brzeziński forgot that Canada did in fact have a minister of state of Polish extraction. Not born in Poland, but undoubtedly Polish.

Stanisław (or Stanley, as he became known later on) Haidasz was born in 1923 in Toronto to a family of Polish immigrants from Stanisławów, a major city in eastern Poland, later to be annexed by the Soviet Union.

Haidasz was an excellent student at St. Michael College School. Upon graduation, he entered a seminary to become a priest with the order of Oblates of Mary Immaculate. During his studies at University of Ottawa, he changed his mind and turned to medicine. After an internship at St. Joseph's Health Centre in Toronto, Haidasz opened a private practice, but remained on call with the St. Joseph's Centre, located in the western end of the city largely inhabited by Polish immigrants, for the next 40 years.

Haidasz was first of all a physician, but very early on he became interested in politics and joined the Liberal Party, successfully running in 1957 for the MP mandate in the Toronto riding of Trinity.

He was defeated a year later in a Conservative landslide that gave power to the government of John Diefenbaker but regained his seat in the 1962 election, winning the seat in the riding of Parkdale, which was partly inhabited by Polish immigrants. Haidasz retained his seat through five succeeding elections until 1978 when he became the first Canadian of Polish descent to be appointed to the Canadian Senate.

Another aspect to Dr. Haidasz's life was his passion for the Internet. An early supporter of technology's benefits, he saw the digital era as a revolutionary period to promote free speech. He recognized the importance of the internet as a powerful tool for education, communication and commerce.

Writing Haidasz's obituary in *The Globe and Mail* in September 2009, Danny Galagher stated:

> In more than 50 years of public life in Ottawa, Stanley Haidasz accomplished much worthy of celebration. He was an active contributor and a witness to many significant Canadian events and turning points in history in the latter half of the 20th century as a Liberal MP and senator.

In an incident that brought together his roles of doctor and politician, he was one of the first four MPs and medical doctors who rushed to the washroom in the Parliamentary gallery on May 18, 1966. Through acrid smoke, Dr. Haidasz saw that no medical help would make a difference to Paul Chartier, a deranged French Canadian who killed himself in a botched attempt to bomb the House of Commons. Fortunately, no one else besides the bomber was injured in the attempt.

A handwritten note Dr. Haidasz attached to one of the many curriculum vitaes retained by the family read: "Entered politics to legislate Medicare for all Canadians."

His son Walter said, "One of his greatest accomplishments was to bring in Medicare. Politics was his way to help the working people. Many of his patients were working class, so health care was very important to him and them."

"The year 1963 was a ground-breaking one for Dr. Haidasz because he would earn the trust of Prime Minister Lester Pearson and begin the first of many stints as a parliamentary secretary to a cabinet minister," said Danny Gallagher in Haidasz's obituary.

Also in 1963, Haidasz undertook another task. On the suggestion of Lester B. Pearson, he was asked to teach English to a young MP from Québec—Jean Chrétien.

In 1972, Prime Minister Pierre Trudeau appointed Haidasz the Minister of State for Multiculturalism, making him the first person of Polish origin to be named a cabinet minister. Haidasz held that position until 1974.

In the Commons, Haidasz introduced or supported legislation for Unemployment Insurance, the Old Age

Supplement, the creation of Petro-Canada and the abolition of the death penalty, among other issues.

"Few people would realize that he had a lot to do with the introduction of the Clean Air Act," said Haidasz's son. That act was approved in 1970 and regulated release of four specific air pollutants: asbestos, lead, mercury and vinyl chloride.

A doctor who delivered hundreds, if not thousands of babies, Haidasz was opposed to abortion, which he fought against in the Commons and as a senator. In various speeches over the years related to contentious debate, he called doctors who did abortions "licensed executioners." Dr. Haidasz introduced four bills that would protect the unborn, and he sponsored eight amendments to the controversial Bill C-43, the Conservative government's abortion bill, which was defeated in the Senate.

In a tribute to Stanley Haidasz, the Honourable Art Eggleton said about his Senate colleague:

> King George VI once stated that the "highest distinction is service to others." That is true not only of the thirty-six and a half years of service in Parliament as an MP, a cabinet minister and then as a senator, but also Doctor Haidasz's 40 years as a physician, serving the people in his Parkdale community in Toronto.... He was a caring and compassionate person, starting with the dedication to his family and, beyond that, to leadership in the Polish community, remembering his roots as the son of Polish immigrants, and, of course, his service to the people of Canada.

And Honourable Peter A. Stollery added: "I think we should remember Stan as a wonderful man—a fine man—but also someone who made a huge contribution to a great change in the way Canadians see themselves."

Canadians are proud of the policy of multiculturalism. Its theory germinated in the specific culture of Canada—the land of immigrants, welcoming (at least in the latter half of the 20th century) people from all corners of the earth. The policy practice, however, owes a lot to Canada's first Minister of State for Multiculturalism, a proud Pole and a proud Canadian at the same time, Senator Stanley Haidasz.

Canadian multiculturalism, unbelievably, has its roots also in Polish political tradition. During the 17th century, when Europe was torn by religious wars, Poland adopted a traditional policy of tolerance; the Catholic kingdom of Poland became a safe haven for exiles persecuted for their faith, whether non-Catholic or non-Christian. Safety offered by the power of Polish kings was so attractive that Poland became a home for numerous people who had to escape other countries in fear for their lives. Traditional Polish tolerance became one of the factors that brought so many persecuted Jews to Poland, as it was one of the few places where they could feel safe and where no anti-Jewish legislation had been adopted.

Twelve years before Prime Minister Pierre Trudeau announced his multicultural policy, another Polish Canadian, Tadeusz Brzezinski, wrote this:

> The principle of "Canadianism" implies that each ethnic group should contribute the maximum of its values to the common spiritual nature of our future Canada. And it follows that the more valuable the contribution,

the greater the advantage in the future.... A Polish Canadian will not enrich Canada through English traditions, even if he knows all of Shakespeare by heart. Canada will expect his contribution to come from Polish culture. Assimilation or discrimination will serve only to impoverish Canada. There may be an official language, but not an official culture. Therefore all ethnic groups can and should participate in the creation of a Canadian culture, thereby contributing to the sense of unity in the nation.

Dr. Stanley Haidasz was the first Canadian senator of Polish origin, but he wasn't the first Canadian politician of Polish origin. That honour is reserved for Aleksander Edward Kierzkowski, a veteran of the November 1830 Uprising who was elected to the first Parliament of the Canadian Confederation in 1867 as a Liberal MP in the St. Jacques riding (Québec).

The second Polish person involved in politics was Maksymilian Głobeński, elected in 1875 as an independent MP in Montagues riding, also in Québec. Both Haidasz and Głobeński were prominent members of the Canadian society of their time. The next person of Polish descent who entered Canadian politics came from a much more modest background.

Jesse Flis was born in Fosston, Saskatchewan. His father, Władysław Flis, came to Canada as a semiliterate farmer. During the Great Depression, the large Flis family moved to Ontario, where Jesse's father first bought a restaurant in Mississauga but subsequently returned to agricultural pursuits when he purchased a 100-acre farm.

Recalling those years, Jesse remembers his family being called "dirty Galicians." As newcomers, they were contemptuously labelled "DPs" and told to "go back where they came from." An understanding for the immigrant's difficult position remained with Jesse throughout his life. Later, as a politician, he would do all he could to assist immigrants and help reunify families. He was also wholeheartedly and positively committed to supporting the Canadian government's policy of multiculturalism.

Jesse attended a teacher's college in Hamilton and continued his studies at the University of Toronto, to graduate from Ontario Institute for Studies in Education. He worked as a teacher in Toronto for over 20 years, gaining valuable practical experience in the field of special education.

During his employment with the board of education, Jesse received a scholarship to study educational systems in other countries. He took his family to Europe, spending time in 15 different countries, with Poland as his base. He chose Poland deliberately so he could learn more about his parents' homeland. He enrolled in a language course at the University of Warsaw and sent his children to a Polish school.

The one-year scholarship helped Jesse Flis in his next endeavour of establishing special educational programs for Toronto's ethnic youth. He helped set up the Heritage Language Program with the Toronto Board of Education, as well as the Special Behavioural Hospital and Institutional Programs.

At a conference of Canadian Polish youth in Winnipeg in 1970, Flis posed the following question to his audience:

What will your contribution to Canada be? It can be very significant if you decide here and now that your cultural heritage is of great value to you. Since you are Canadians of Polish descent, your cultural heritage can make for a much more colourful Canada. Since you are Canadians and you support the Canadian Government's foreign policy toward Poland, I ask you: what do you plan to do to relay this Polish Canadian identity to your fellow citizens?

Flis indicated that the concept of multiculturalism and its policies provided the best possible platform for collective action or the good of the nation. Only through activities of a cultural nature was it possible to delve deeper into Canadian life and Canadian society. Flis underlined the importance of education, which is the best, most certain personal investment for success in all areas of public life.

In 1979 Flis took up a challenge of direct involvement in Canadian politics, vying for a parliamentary mandate in Toronto's Parkdale riding, vacated by Dr. Stanley Haidasz when the elder statesman was named to the Senate. Flis was elected by a narrow margin of less than 100 votes. The margin was much wider a year later when he defeated the Conservative candidate by over 5000 votes.

Jesse Flis' major goal in Ottawa was helping newcomers to Canada, but he never forgot his ties to Poland and the matter of defending human rights. When martial law was declared in Poland in 1981, Flis, as a member and an MP from the Liberal Party, did not hesitate to criticize Prime Minister Trudeau for his opinion that "martial law is better than civil war." John Crosbie, the Opposition's External Affairs critic, called Flis a "Polish Pimpernel" for trying to make the Polish affair a separate motion. In October 1982, on a motion from Flis, the House of Commons unanimously condemned the delegalization of the Independent Free Trade Union "Solidarity" in Poland and the decision to introduce martial law in the country.

In 1997, Flis retired from political life. He considered his job well done. "After working 27 years in education and 14 years in politics, I guess it is about time to devote my energies to family and friends," he said.

The contribution of Polish Canadians to the development of Canada is not widely known or recognized. This is because Polish Canadians do not seem to be very active in promoting their contributions. Some efforts to change this, however, have been made recently.

In 2009, the Polish Canadian Women's Federation organized the exhibition "Polish Sprit" to present the achievements of Canadians of Polish origin who have made significant contributions to Ontario's heritage in community work, politics, culture, science and engineering. The exhibition was partly based on a list of 60 Polish Canadians of note. The list, although composed under the guidance of a special nominating committee of prominent members of the Polish community, is obviously arbitrary. It may, however, serve as an indication of the extent and variety of the fields where Polish contribution to Canadian success may be found.

Janusz (John) A. Brzozowski was born in Warsaw, Poland. He received a bachelor and a masters degree of science in electrical engineering from the University of Toronto in 1957 and 1959, respectively, and masters and postdoctoral degrees in electrical engineering from

Princeton University in 1962. He was assistant professor (1962–65) and associate professor (1965–67) in the Department of Electrical Engineering at the University of Ottawa. From 1967 to 1996, he was a professor in the Department of Computer Science and also held a cross-appointment in the Department of Electrical and Computer Engineering at the University of Waterloo.

In the periods 1978 to 1983 and from 1987 to 1989, he was chair of the University of Waterloo's Department of Computer Science. He had visiting appointments at the University of California, Berkeley (1965–66), University of Paris (1974–75), University of Sao Paulo (1983), Kyoto University (1984) and Eindhoven University (1989–90). Dr. Brzozowski has published many papers in the areas of theory of languages and automata, asynchronous circuits, and testing. He is co-author of *Digital Networks* (1976) and of *Asynchronous Circuits* (1995). His present research interests include automata and formal languages.

As difficult as it is to assess the contribution of Brzozowski's specialized work, an entry in Wikipedia comments on his contribution in the area of formal languages: "there are today at least three concepts bearing Brzozowski's name in honour of his contributions…" Obviously, specialists in his field acknowledged his achievements, and that is why he can proudly state that he was awarded, among others, such prestigious academic honours as Distinguished Professor Emeritus, University of Waterloo, and the Canadian Pioneer in Computing Award. There were only 40 recipients of the pioneer award in 2005. In the introduction at the awards ceremony, Dr. Kelly Lyons, director at the IBM Centre of Advanced Studies in Toronto, stated:

> By honouring these Pioneers, we're also acknowledging the extraordinary impact they have had on the evolution of the Canadian computing industry over the last 50 years. We want to ensure that these Pioneers' place in Canadian computer science history is recognized and documented, so that young people will be inspired to follow in their footsteps.

Another Polish immigrant to Canada of the time, Tomir Bałut, made his way to this country in an unorthodox manner. Born in 1927, he fought in the Polish resistance—the famous Home Army. After the war, he tried to adapt to new conditions in a country taken over by the Communists, but he finally decided he'd had enough, and in October 1950 he escaped to Sweden by flying a training plane. From Sweden he immigrated to Canada and started working in the aerospace industry in Montréal. In 1956 he moved to Toronto to complete his studies and later worked for Ontario Hydro. His first interest concentrated on turbines, but in 1963 he became interested in nuclear energy and received a licence from the Atomic Energy Control Board to manage a nuclear reactor. He spent the next three years in India, working as an engineer on the Rajasthan Atomic Power Project.

It would be wrong to think that the Poles who found their place in Canada were mainly engineers and pilots. Jan Józef Marek Brancewicz came to Canada in 1965 with an unusual profession of poet. His poetry was widely published in Poland and was also translated into German. In Canada, Brancewicz modified his artistic interests somewhat and took up painting and art instruction. In an introduction to the Clear Lake Festival, its founder, Professor Alexander Tselyakov, wrote of his Polish colleague:

> Jan Brancewicz is an internationally recognized artist specializing in oil painting and printmaking. For over 20 years he investigated medium of digital printmaking and his works were exhibited in most prestigious international exhibition of prints in Krakow, Poland. For over 30 years he was instructor of painting and design at Brandon University.... His main interest is investigating human conditions and their relations to the natural organic and man-made environments. He believes that the impact of urban environment is dehumanizing, and makes us to perform like machines.

Jan Brancewicz was a member of the Manitoba Arts Council and liked to point out that his works really reached the world—they are exhibited in galleries on five continents. He retired from teaching in 2006. He is still involved in mentoring young artists and works as art director for Bear Paw Publishing and *Canadian Journal of Native Studies*.

Another unusual Polish Canadian biography is that of Henryk E. Mindak. The sheer size of Canada would force the country to be a haven for map-making. It is, however, a much more complex task than you might imagine. Creating maps requires both knowledge and imagination. Mindak was one of the few Canadian cartographers. Born in Poland, he immigrated to Ottawa in 1951. He was offered a cartographic position with the Department of Energy, Mines and Resources, Surveys and Mapping Branch. From 1951 to 1964 he was responsible for a great variety of cartographic projects, including mathematical computations for map projection, research, compilation and design of Special Purpose Maps. He compiled and designed the first edition maps of New Brunswick (published in 1962), Northern Hemisphere (1965), and The Northwest Territory And Yukon Territory (1966).

In 1963, Mindak researched, compiled and designed a modern world projection map entitled *The World*. With the assistance of 11 other cartographers, he planned, compiled and designed the first edition of a completely new *International Map of the World*, which was produced to United Nations specifications and published in 1965. In the following years, 74 maps were published, covering the whole of Canada, with uniform scale coverage. In addition, he designed a map of Canada showing its relationship to Europe over the North Pole and the relationship of Canada to that of Australia and South America over the South Pole.

In December 1964, Mindak was promoted to the position of chief cartographer in the geographical branch of the department. In this capacity he was responsible for the planning, design, cartographic execution and editorial approval of cartography for the *National Atlas of Canada*.

For Canada's centennial year in 1967, he designed a new "Territorial Evolution of Canada" map sheet, which was made of 23 smaller maps covering the years 1667 to 1949. He used 27 brilliant colour tints and designed a decorative red maple leaf map border for this celebration.

At that time, *The Chronicle-Herald* in Halifax placed a large and bold heading in its paper: "Henry Mindak's Map Traces Canada's Birth." The report accentuated "the Polish born cartographer..." Dr. Izabella Jost, who was dedicated to this project, did the historical research for this map. In 1974, the *National Atlas of Canada* and *L'Atlas National Du Canada* were published with 245 pages of maps and diagrams and over 230 colour tints.

In 1976, Mindak was invited to Rideau Hall in Ottawa, where His Excellency The Right Honourable Jules Leger, Governor General of Canada at the time, presented him with the Gold Medal, awarded by the Royal Canadian Geographical Society to the Honourable Alastair W. Gillespie, Minister of Energy, Mines and Resources, and the team of more than 40 individuals responsible for the production of the *National Atlas of Canada*. One of the recipients was Henry Mindak.

Mindak designed maps for the *Geographical Map Series* and other maps such as *Canada Relief, Lakes, Rivers And Glaciers, Canada Energy, Census Divisions* and *International Relations*. For the Pan-American Institute of Geography and History, he designed *America Latina, Mapa General De Transportes*, published in 1968, and for the Royal Canadian Mounted Police Centennial 1873–1973, he partially recreated an 1888 map of *Mounted Police Stations & Patrols In North-West Territories*, published in 1973.

Henryk Mindak became a cartographic editor and worked with Mr. J.M.O. Morawiecki, who was a research editor. After six years of planning and design, the *Canada Gazetteer Atlas* and *Canada Atlas*

Toponymique were published in 1980, with 96 pages of shaded relief maps and 13,000 physical features with roads, railways, national and provincial parks and with 22,000 populated places. In 1981 he designed and published a new *Colour Progression Chart* showing over 200 colour tints for the future generation of cartographers.

Henryk Mindak won three public service awards and four certificates of excellence granted by the Technical Publication and Graphic Art competitions. He was the co-founder of the Ontario Institute of Chartered Cartographers, Ottawa Branch, and was a Fellow of the Royal Geographical Society, London, England.

In 1955, a book publishing company from Toronto approached Professor B. Zaborski, head of the geography department at the University of Ottawa, requesting the names of graduates willing to produce maps for historical and geographical textbooks and atlases. There were no volunteers. With great hesitation, Henryk Mindak accepted the offer and produced over 1000 maps, which were published in scientific journals, books and atlases.

Most of the Polish Canadians mentioned above made their careers in Ontario. Most, but not all.

Established in 1967 by Her Majesty Queen Elizabeth II, the Order of Canada is the centrepiece of Canada's honours system and recognizes a lifetime of outstanding achievement, dedication to the community and service to the nation. The Order recognizes people in all sectors of Canadian society. Their contributions are varied, yet they have all enriched the lives of others and made a difference to this country. On May 3, 2007, the Order of Canada was awarded to

Professor Zbigniew Kabata of Nanaimo, British Columbia.

Zbigniew Kabata was one more of the innumerable veterans of the war Nazi Germany led on all fronts in Europe and the world, but most bitterly fought on Polish land. Like scores of his countrymen, Kabata joined the Polish Underground, or Home Army, to fight the invading German armies, although in 1939, he was barely 15 years old. Honoured and decorated for his bravery in combat with the unit that gained fame for raids on Nazi jails to free Polish prisoners, Kabata escaped the approaching Soviet forces and joined the famous II Corps to fight in Tobruk in North Africa. Demobilized in Britain, he started his civilian life as a deckhand on a North Sea trawler, which grew into his fascination with maritime zoology and studies at the University of Aberdeen. In September 1953, Kabata, who was at that time an undergraduate student, married an Irish physician, Mary Ann Montgomery. The couple's daughter, Marta, was born in 1954, and their son, Andrzej, in 1956.

In 1967, the Kabata family moved to the Pacific Biological Station in Nanaimo, British Columbia. Zbigniew Kabata became the station head of the Marine Fisheries Section. His list of achievements exceeds the space limits imposed on this book, but he is a world-renowned expert on marine parasitology and his work has been acknowledged with patronymy of 22 taxa, including most notably, the copepod, *Bobkabata kabatabobus*. He is a scientist, a teacher and a veteran with the rank of lieutenant colonel, but he is also a fisherman and a poet. The poem "Underground Army," composed during his service in the Polish

Resistance, became the unofficial anthem of the Home Army community and is inscribed on countless monuments honouring their heroism.

The Law Society of Canada, Immigration Branch, granted Kabata a newly established Immigrant Achievement Award in April 2002. In 2007, he became a Member of the Order of Canada. The citation for the order reads:

> Zbigniew Kabata is an internationally renowned authority on the biology of marine parasites, and was the long-standing head of parasitology research at the Pacific Biological Station in Nanaimo. His groundbreaking research, spanning over five decades, has greatly improved our understanding of marine ecology and has had a significant worldwide impact on the management of commercial fisheries. Undeterred by retirement, he actively pursues his research and remains an eminent authority in this important field of biological study.

Most of the information on Polish Canadians in this book is based on secondary sources. There are almost one million Polish Canadians in this country, and it is rarely that a historian has an opportunity to personally meet the subjects of his work. I have a personal reason to include here a brief note about Karol Krótki, a noted demographer and an expert on Canadian ethnic issues. Decades ago, when I was still a teenager, I happened to meet Professor Krótki in, of all places, Karachi, Pakistan. I was there with my family, as my father was at the time working for the embassy of Poland to Pakistan. Krótki was one of the few Polish people living in Karachi. I do not think he would remember the lanky teenager who had no idea whom he was speaking with, and I only remembered him as one of the first examples confirming the theory that there is no place on Earth where it is impossible to find traces of Poland and its people.

Krótki was another in a long line of Poles thrown out of their country by the events of World War II. He escaped to Hungary, then to France, where he joined the Polish Armed Forces to fight at Tobruk with the legendary Carpathian Brigade. From 1943 he could be found among the Polish fliers fighting the Nazi Luftwaffe on all fronts.

Like many of his comrades in arms, Krótki stayed in Britain when the war ended. He worked at a Chivers marmalade plant and completed his university studies at Cambridge University, receiving a Master of Arts degree in economics, with statistics, in 1952. Eight years later he complemented it with a PhD in Economics from Princeton. In the meantime, he worked as a statistician in Sudan, and in Karachi (1960–64) as an advisor to the Institute of Economic Development, a UN agency. Later years took him to several U.S. universities (Berkeley, Chapel Hill, Ann Arbor), and the two years he spent in Morocco let him acquire exceptional expertise in the matter of demography of Muslim countries.

In 1964, Krótki settled in Canada, accepting the position of professor of demographics at the University of Alberta. From there he supervised the work of several graduate students, published 12 books and over 130 scientific publications on demographics, ethnic affairs and immigration. Krótki was a member (in the years 1981–84, as president) of the Canadian

Population Society, and from 1988 he was on the board of Statistics Canada. In 1979 he was elected a fellow of the Royal Society of Canada.

To quote from his obituary published in 2007 by the University of Alberta:

> Dr. Krotki was a larger than life figure, bringing his international experiences in the academy, government, and the military, and his fluency in several languages, into the classroom and the department meetings.... Many of the graduate students Dr. Krotki mentored are today established professors in major universities or are employed in senior positions in important demographic institutes. He was a key figure in the creation of the Population Research Laboratory and the journal Canadian Studies in Population, and in the design of several demographic surveys that are still considered to be landmark studies. He also brought into being The Society of Edmonton Demographers, an organization that over the years has raised thousands of dollars in support of demographic research in the Sociology department.

For years I had planned to try to meet Professor Karol Krótki on my next visit to Edmonton. Regretfully, it never happened. All that remains for me is the memory of a brief meeting in Karachi of a Polish teenager and a Polish scientist, who years later would both become Canadians.

Science, industry, engineering—these are the fields where an immigrant may excel and become prominent in his or her new homeland, given talent and having braved the necessity of hard work. It is usually much more difficult to achieve recognition in the field of the arts or the media. Mark Starowicz, however, proved that the accomplishment was possible.

Starowicz was born in 1946 in England to Polish parents who immigrated to Montréal in 1954. Mark completed his studies at the McGill University and joined the staff of *The Montréal Gazette* in 1964 as a reporter. He continued his career with *The Toronto Star* and the CBC. From 1982 to 1992, he was the executive producer of the CBC TV newsmagazine program, *The Journal*. He was also the executive producer of the 2000 TV mini-series, *Canada: A People's History*. Starowicz was made an Officer of the Order of Canada in 2004 for having "demonstrated and shared his pride in Canada."

As a journalist and a producer, Mark Starowicz has transformed the Canadian broadcasting industry and produced some of this country's most influential current affairs and documentary programs. An articulate and outspoken advocate of Canadian culture and identity, he has immeasurably enriched our collective experience and inspired two generations of documentary filmmakers with his vision, ingenuity and dedication.

The ultimate expression of Starowicz's creativity and passion for Canadian history and culture is his monumental 32-hour documentary series *Canada: A People's History*. Airing over two years in both English and French, the series attracted over 14 million viewers and won three Gemini Awards, capturing the imagination of Canadians everywhere and establishing an enduring and inspiring national legacy. The film has been translated into seven languages and is used in thousands of schools across Canada. "There is a persistent idea that Canadians aren't interested in their own stories," said Starowicz. "I've made a living proving it is not true."

Mark Starowicz has honorary degrees from six Canadian universities. Not bad for the son of immigrants.

One of the few Polish Canadian artists who gained fame in Canada is Professor Walter Buczyński, born in Toronto to a Polish immigrant family. He is a Canadian pianist and composer, but his work also indicates strong ties to the culture of his parents' homeland. He studied piano with Earle Moss and composition with Godfrey Ridout, at Aspen with Darius Milhaud and Charles Jones, and Rosina Lhévinne (New York, 1958–59) and Zbigniew Drzewiecki (Warsaw, 1959 and 1961), and, for composition, with Nadia Boulanger (Paris, 1960 and 1962).

From 1962 to 1969, Buczyński taught piano and theory at the Royal Conservatory of Music of Toronto. He also began teaching these same subjects, and composition, at the University of Toronto in 1969. During the 1960s and early 1970s, he gave solo concerts in New York, Paris, Warsaw and many Canadian cities, as well as performed recitals on CBC radio, featuring his own and other contemporary Canadian works in addition to his standard repertoire. He was president of the Canadian League of Composers.

Buczyński's music of the late 1960s and early 1970s often leaned on satire or whimsy. The *Zeroing In* series included multimedia elements such as spatial movement, mime and spoken phrases. The short chamber opera *From the Buczynski Book of the Living*, to the composer's own libretto, poked fun at R. Murray Schafer's *From the Tibetan Book of the Dead*.

In 1977, Buczyński received the Queen Elizabeth Silver Jubilee medal, and in 1992, he was the recipient of the Governor General's 125th Anniversary of Confederation of Canada medal for his contribution to Canadian cultural achievement.

As mentioned earlier, the list composed by the Polish Canadian Women's Federation for the Polish Spirit exhibition was arbitrary. My choice of prominent Polish Canadians presented in this chapter is equally, if not more, arbitrary and incomplete. We could carry on almost endlessly this review of biographies of prominent or deserving Canadians of Polish origin who devoted their talents and work to their new country. Musicians and biologists, teachers and engineers, scientists and activists work tirelessly to make their new home better.

Daria Haust, a professor of pathology and one of the founders of pediatric pathology, was the first woman to be appointed to the Medical Faculty of the Queen's University in Kingston, and she was the first president of the Canadian Atherosclerosis Society.

Jerzy Dobrowolski of Ottawa developed thin film anti-counterfeiting security devices safeguarding Canadian banknotes.

Professor Jerzy Wojciechowski was a philosopher who taught in Montréal and St. Francis Xavier University in Nova Scotia, specializing in philosophy of science and nature. He was appointed the First Honorary Life Member of the Canadian Philosophical Association.

Paweł Wyczyński, a literary historian, became an expert in French Canadian literature, who, in the words of *The Ottawa Citizen*, introduced the world to French Canadian writing.

Marianna Sikorska, a principal research officer at the National Research Council in Ottawa, is considered a groundbreaking researcher in fundamental cell biology and neurobiology.

These are just a few examples of the contributions Polish Canadians made or are continuously making to the growth, prosperity and further development of Canada. The prosperous era after the war changed Canada beyond recognition. Gone was the country ravaged by the Great Depression, the country relying on its staple exports of wheat and minerals. In its place was a nation well prepared to experience a period of unimaginable development.

The extraordinary growth of Canada in the post-war period gave Canadians the second highest standard of living in the world. Production reached record levels in all sectors of the economy. Development of new resources also proceeded on an unimaginable scale.

But these changes did not happen overnight. Some 20 years were needed to launch the process on its irreversible course and to ensure it did not slow down in the coming decades. The changes that took place in the post-war period are mind-boggling.

Between 1945 and 1966, the population of the country grew by about 60 percent. In 1941 the urban population of Canada represented barely over 50 percent of the total number of the inhabitants of the country; by 1961, three quarters of Canadians lived in towns and cities, and farming was the main source of income for less than 20 percent of Canadians. Between 1951 and 1965, mineral production of Canada grew threefold, the value of manufactured goods grew two-fold and generated electricity threefold. In 1951 there were 2.8 million vehicles registered in Canada; 15 years later, that number grew to almost 6.7 million.

On the eve of World War II, the gross national product of Canada was calculated at $5.6 billion; by 1967 the value had climbed to $60 billion. The average weekly industrial wage of Canadians in 1945 was $32; in 1965 it grew to $93.

The changes affected not only the tangible—urbanization, industry, education, and so on—but also the intangibles, for example, the feeling of achievement and of having played a role in world affairs and having played it well. Canadian cities became an exciting place to live; Canadian artists showed their mettle on the world stage; and Canadians lived fuller and happier lives. Most Canadians quickly accepted this state of affairs; it was only the politicians who still were haunted by the memories of the Great Depression.

The lifestyle of the baby boomers changed and pushed Canada into the foremost position in the world. Canadians devoted more years to attaining an education, and they married, bore and raised children at a younger age. The young affluent society purchased more consumer goods, more houses, more automobiles. The real estate market became a more important factor of the economy than before the war. The recreation market—the tourist industry serving both the foreign and the domestic consumer—became an economic factor, not just a subject for social gossip. In September 1966, the population of the country reached 20 million; it was predicted that by the end of the 20th century, Canada would have 40 million inhabitants.

Most of this growth was the result of natural increase. Immigration, however, should not be discounted. After all, in 1957 the number of immigrants to Canada reached a record level of 282,000 people, accounting for one-fourth of the total population growth. Most of the immigrants came from the British Isles, supplemented by newcomers form Italy, Greece and Portugal. The Polish immigrants were not numerous in this army of new Canadians. As the stories in this chapter show, however, the Poles contributed to the expansion of Canada with their talent, experience and hard work.

CHAPTER EIGHT

MORE THAN JUST
PEROGIES

The latest wave of Polish immigrants to reach
Canadian shores was once again completely
different from the earlier ones. It is often
referred to as "the Solidarity wave," because it appeared
in the 1980s as a result of the crackdown by the Communist authorities in Poland against the free trade
union movement born in Gdańsk shipyards. The
movement ultimately generated social conditions that
led to the overthrow of the Communist regime in
Poland and, indirectly, in other Eastern European
countries and finally in the Soviet Union itself. The
final overthrow of Communist authorities in Poland
came almost a decade later, however, and in the winter
of 1981, not many people in Poland truly believed it
could be achieved.

Regulations regarding foreign travel in the last years
before the birth of the Solidarity Movement, and

during the 18 months of "Solidarity" before the crack-down caused the introduction of martial law in Poland, were relaxed. A relatively large number of Solidarity activists and people close to the movement were in fact outside Poland's borders on December 13, 1981. The inability of the Communist regime to control international travel allowed other illegal émigrés to escape Poland, even after the introduction of martial law.

Finally, within months of its last attempt at controlling the country, the Communist regime realized that its days were numbered and tried to prolong the agony by "exporting" some of the most vocal and respected "Solidarity" activists. An unheard of document was invented, contrary to both the theory and the practice in consular affairs up to this date: Polish citizens were given permission to leave Poland on the condition that they had been issued a special travel document. Their passports, which in diplomatic and consular practice were always an indication that the issuing country accepts responsibility for the bearer of the document and extends its consular care over him or her, were stamped with an inscription: "Not valid for return journey to the country of issue."

The Solidarity wave was comprised of political activists "exported" outside Poland's borders, of people who did not wait and struggle for true independence of Poland from the Communists, and of people who were trapped beyond their homeland by the events of December 13 and were afraid to go back to their country because of a distinct possibility of Soviet intervention on the mode of the summer of 1968 in Czechoslovakia. The wave also included—particularly in the first half of the 1980s—people who were accidentally dispersed all over the world by the historic events, even though they had no preconceived intention of changing their country of residence.

The history of that wave of immigrants has still to be written. Whatever statements and conclusions are being made here, they are the result of personal observations and attempts at quantifying general information from a still dispersed mass of data. It is, and still has to be, an attempt at indicating trends rather than describing reality.

The size of the "Solidarity" wave of immigrants is still a matter under discussion. Provisional estimates vary from 500,000 to two million people leaving Poland between 1981 and 1989 and settling in various countries. Canada accepted about 80,000 of these immigrants.

Whether we take the lower or the higher number as closer to fact, it has to be stressed that approximately half of these immigrants sooner or later returned to Poland. Once again, there is little reliable statistical data regarding the flow of Polish immigrants to and from Canada, but partial data supports a theory that Canada proved somewhat more welcoming to this wave of immigrants than other accepting countries.

In 1982–83 there were practically five countries of the world, more or less readily accepting Polish refugees: the United States, Canada, Australia, New Zealand and South Africa. With the exception of the U.S., these countries were considered exotic to the Polish refugees stranded in France, Germany, Italy, Austria, Greece and other European countries.

In 1987, I had a long conversation with one of the Solidarity activists "exported" out of Poland with a one-way passport. He was offered asylum in Canada, and he selected Vancouver as his preferred place of residence. As he said, "It was as far away from the Russians as I could get." In his opinion, if the Soviet armies ever started their march, it would be in Europe to the west, and not from Siberia to the east.

Thus, he and his family arrived in Vancouver, were greeted kindly at the airport and taken to a hotel to rest after a long journey. "Tomorrow, we will go out to see the town," promised my acquaintance to his family. The next morning it was raining, as it often is in Vancouver. "We'll go sightseeing tomorrow," promised the father. The story repeated itself on the third day, the fourth, and the fifth.... Apparently, as he told me, it was a rainy month in Vancouver, with lighter or heavier rainfalls for 24 days in a row. I never got to verify this information with Environment Canada, but it seems plausible. On the 24th day of rain, the family decided they'd had enough. "We are not frogs; let's ask the authorities for a resettlement to another city." On the 25th day, the sun was shining, and they finally went sightseeing in their new home. There was no more talk of moving anywhere else. As far as I know, they still live in Vancouver.

The story illustrates two key characteristics of the Solidarity wave of immigrants. First, they were not familiar with their new countries of residence, in spite of their relatively high level of education and some experience with foreign travel. Second, they were not forced to seek any asylum for the homeless, as was the case with the veterans of World War II and the DPs of the 1940s. They could not or would not go back to Poland, but they were not at the mercy of

circumstances. They felt better in their new homelands and, as a rule, demonstrated a different attitude
to those countries, particularly to Canada. There
were fewer tendencies to hide in an ethnic ghetto, such
as in Chicago in the United States. The Solidarity
refugees were more open to the world, more willing to
participate in the life of their adopted homelands and
quicker to realize the potential of their professional
and civic experience.

According to Dr. Anna Reczyńska from Jagiellonian
University in Cracow, the foremost Polish expert on
the history of Polish Canadians, the "Solidarity" wave
of Polish immigrants to Canada numbered about
80,000 people in the years 1981 to 1991, and a further 35,000 Polish immigrants taken in by Canada in
the years 1991 to 1996. The people arriving in this
wave were relatively young, well educated and usually
able to communicate in one of the official languages of
their new country. The end of the wave occurred in the
late 1990s. The Polish community in Canada stopped
growing and was relegated out, by other ethnic communities, as the first 10 sources of new Canadians.

According to Statistics Canada, 265,930 Canadians
declared themselves to be of Polish origin in 1996 (the
1996 census changed the method of assigning ethnic
origin, which accounts for the large disparity between
the 1996 figure and the 2006 figure of almost one million). A comparison of these figures (1996 and 2006
Census data, and Dr. Reczyńska's assessment of the
number of immigrants in the 1980s and 1990s) leads
to a conclusion that the "Solidarity" wave of immigrants became an important factor in the further
development of the Polish community in this country.

Polish Canadians tend to concentrate in Ontario (about 60 percent of the total Polish Canadian population, based on 1996 data). Unfortunately, at the time of this writing, the 2006 census data on this subject was not yet available. The second province in this ranking is Alberta (almost 30,000 Polish Canadians) and then British Columbia (about 25,000). Québec and Manitoba follow with approximately 20,000 and 17,000 Polish Canadians, respectively.

The immigrants of the 1980s settled predominantly in Ontario. It is obvious, therefore, that such a sizeable influx of "new blood" changed the face of the Polish Canadian community in this part of the country. The older Polish Canadians were more or less content to remain a separate community within the Canadian ethnic mosaic. The new immigrants wanted to join Canadian society on an equal footing with members of established communities. They knew their worth and, mostly, had no fear of their strange new circumstances.

Obviously, such a basic difference in their approach to the Canadian reality led to numerous conflicts. First of all within Polish Canadian organizations. As a rule, such organizations play the role of supplying self-help resources to a community feeling estranged in a new land. Traditional Polish Canadian organizations were such a source of assistance, where one could either seek direct help with a small practical matter or rely on to provide comradeship and national feeling of comfort through celebrations and practice of social life "like in the old country." The new wave of immigrants accepted all these aspects of Polish Canadian life, but asked for more. They wanted the organizations to become a bridge connecting the community to every-day Canadian life. They wanted an equal opportunity not only with other ethnic communities but also with the Anglo-Saxon (or French, in Québec) reality of Canada.

One of the leading organizations in this respect is the Association of Polish Engineers in Canada. It has always played a mediatory role between the Polish immigrants and the Canadian reality, and the effects of its activity during its 70 years of existence deserve a more detailed description. Today, the organization is alive and well, dynamically active where others are often a moribund remnant of former glory. From the beginning, the association served as a path to professional Canada for its members; it bore fruit for them, for the organization and for the community as a whole.

The other organization deserving mention in this context is the Polish Alliance of Canada (PAC), created in 1924. Currently, it is the largest Polish organization in Canada, and throughout the years it has successfully navigated a winding course of assisting Polish immigrants to settle in Canada and of helping the country recognize the possibility of contribution from its Polish newcomers. The role of the organization is shown in a series of 26 paintings by William Kurelek, a noted Canadian artist, entitled *The Polish Canadians*. The series, illustrating Polish settlers' lives, was commissioned by the PAC and executed by the artist just prior to his death in 1977. The paintings were subsequently presented by the Alliance as a gift to the Art Gallery of Hamilton, where they are now part of the gallery's permanent collection.

Both of these organizations date back to the era of World War II, and their activity follows programs and fulfils needs established at that time. The last 30 years saw a basic change in the relationship of Polish Canadians with their new homeland. In the Greater Toronto Area, it is most evident in the geography of the community. In 1981, the centre of Polish presence in Toronto was located on Roncesvalles Avenue in the western part of the city. That was the location of the "Polish bank" or St. Stanislaus–St. Casimir's Polish Parishes Credit Union, numerous food stores offering Polish or Polish-style products, travel agencies specializing in travel to the homeland or shipping of packages for families in Poland, Polish restaurants and so on. By 2010, the largest Polish financial institution outside Poland has 18 branches in Ontario, including Brampton, Guelph, Hamilton, Kitchener, London, Oshawa and Windsor, but only four of them are located close to the old Polish neighbourhood on Roncesvalles Avenue; four new ones were created in Mississauga.

It is Mississauga, the sixth largest city in Canada (by population), that is today the centre of Polish Canadian presence in the GTA. And the presence has a different quality to it than 25 years ago. For example, there are two Polish supermarkets in Mississauga operating under the name "Starsky." Both stores started as bigger, more luxurious versions of traditional sources of Polish products. Both stores are truly supermarkets, offering a different quality shopping experience than the traditional "mom-and-pop" stores conventional to all ethnic communities in Canada and other countries.

Starsky is as Polish as Longo's is Italian—and is Canadian at the same time. It started as a supermarket mainly for the Polish Canadian clientele; within a year of opening, probably at least half of its customers did not speak Polish. Starsky introduced an interesting innovation in retail trade: its floor personnel wear name badges with important additional information: "I speak English and…" When the store opened, most badges read at the end of this phrase "Polish," "Russian" or "Ukrainian." Today, one can find badges declaring additional spoken languages such as, for example, Arabic.

Polish cuisine is not widely known or popular in Canada. It would seem that Starsky is doing all it can, and with good results, to change the perception that Polish food equals a stack of perogies.

Mississauga was chosen as a location for the Catholic church of St. Maximilian Kolbe and its adjoining Polish Cultural Centre. The old Polish House in the heart of Toronto, on Beverley Street, is slowly dying, but the Mississauga Centre is vibrant and dynamic as a site of cultural activity. The centre provides weekly films or events such as the festival of Polish sea shanties attended by fans of this specific genre of pop culture, regardless of their ethnic origin. What is more, the centre in Mississauga has become truly Canadian—a large number of events hosted by the centre have nothing to do with Poland. The centre offers its facilities to other ethnic communities as well, while Polish-organized events quite often take place nowadays in such purely Canadian venues as, for example, The Rose Theatre in Brampton.

Believe it or not, the Polish Canadian community in the GTA boasts of its own professional theatre. Operating under the name of Music and Poetry Salon, it is the labour of love of one family. Its existence and success, however, proves that the Polish community does not treat its stay in Canada as temporary or accidental. We are at home, and we like theatre, so let's organize it, support it and bring lively cultural events to our life in Canada.

The Salon became a fact thanks to the tireless efforts of two women, Maria Nowotarska and her daughter Agata Pilitowska, both of whom were professional actresses in Poland before coming to Canada. Instrumental to its success was also the husband and father of the two artists, the general manager of the Salon (or rather its *spiritus movens*) Jerzy Pilitowski. His achievements deserve recognition.

Born in Kalisz, the oldest Polish city mentioned in Ancient Roman chronicles, Jerzy Pilitowski entered the world stage during World War II as a resistance courier (he was 15 at that time) and later as a member of the Polish Scouting resistance formation known as "Grey Ranks," the name taken from the grey colour of their peacetime uniforms. He fought in the Warsaw Uprising of 1944 and ended up in a prisoner of war camp near Dresden. Together with his friends, Jerzy escaped and got through the lines to the American units, to join the legendary Polish II Corps. Demobilized in London, he somehow managed to establish contact with his family back in Poland and, in spite of the Communist threat, decided to return home. The re-established family moved to Kraków, where Jerzy took up university studies in architecture. As Kraków is near the highest mountain range in Poland (the Tatra Mountains), Jerzy also became an avid climber.

In 1956 in Kraków, a student cabaret was established under the name of *Piwnica pod Baranami* (The Cellar Under the Rams). It quickly became a major cultural force in Poland in music, poetry, fine arts, song and other media. Jerzy was one of the organizers of the cabaret from its start. His future wife, Maria, was one of the actors, but his own role in the cabaret was always in the background. Apparently, he could not sing as well as he wished; he was paralyzed by stage fright and generally felt more comfortable cleaning up, organizing and decorating. As the cabaret relied on the goodwill of people ready to work for nothing, Jerzy played a major role in its success. His experience in organizing stage productions came in handy 35 years later in Canada.

In the meantime, Jerzy graduated from university and started working as an architect. He specialized in urban planning, and a few small towns near Krakow owe him their charm and lifestyle. Finally, his team of architects and urban planners won an invitation to tender the reconstruction of the Iraqi capital Baghdad.

In 1986, after the Chernobyl disaster, Jerzy's grown-up daughter Agata decided she did not want her three children to live in a radioactive environment, and she managed to move to Canada. Three years later, Jerzy and Maria visited Toronto to see their daughter and became Canadian immigrants.

In Toronto, Jerzy met his wartime friend Wojtek Wronski, who at the time was employed as a municipal planner by the city administration. The Pilitowski family was suddenly established in their new country.

Soon, however, artistic passion proved stronger than the demands of everyday life. Jerzy, Maria and Agata started dreaming of some form of theatrical enterprise to enliven the cultural atmosphere of Polish Ontario. It all started at the University of Toronto Hart House, whose evening shows concentrated on music. Soon, the three members of the family added poetry recitals, and the Salon of Music and Poetry moved to the Old Mill hall, to the Centre in Mississauga, and finally to a professional standard theatre in the Mississauga Public Library on Burnhamthorpe Road.

The demands of the theatre quickly made the former soldier, mountaineer, architect and urban planner change his profession once more, to that of theatre manager. He occasionally appeared on stage, but his first duty was managing the theatre, and he let his wife and daughter shine as its stars.

In December 2006, a special show was held in the theatre presenting the Christmas atmosphere of Kraków, the Polish cultural capital and a celebrated city central to most Polish cultural traditions. There were four actors on stage: Maria Nowotarska, Agata Pilitowska, Jerzy's and Maria's son Piotr Pilitowski (who lives in Poland and was performing in Toronto as a guest of the salon) and Agata's son Maciek Lis. Three generations of one family in the same theatrical premiere. It was a momentous evening for Jerzy Pilitowski and for the Polish Canadian community, which can truly be proud of its theatre.

Polish "high art" in Canada is not limited to theatre. Let's take a look at the musical scene. Anyone familiar with piano music in Canada must have heard of Janina Fialkowska, probably the best interpreter of Chopin's music anywhere in the country today. Born in Montréal to a Canadian mother and Polish father, Janina has been charming her audiences for over 30 years. A reviewer of *La Presse* described her as "an artist of rare distinction." She is also greatly valued by experts for familiarizing Canadian audiences with contemporary 20th-century Polish music.

She has performed with the foremost North American orchestras, among them the Chicago Symphony, the Cleveland Orchestra, the Los Angeles Philharmonic, the Philadelphia Orchestra, the Houston Symphony and the Pittsburgh Symphony as well as with all of the principal Canadian orchestras, including the Montréal Symphony Orchestra, the Toronto Symphony Orchestra, the National Arts Centre Orchestra of Ottawa, the Calgary Philharmonic and the Vancouver Symphony Orchestra.

Fialkowska has appeared as guest artist with the Royal Concertgebouw Orchestra of Amsterdam, the Halle Orchestra, the London Philharmonic, London's Philharmonia Orchestra, the BBC Symphony, the Royal Philharmonic, the Scottish National Orchestra, the Warsaw Philharmonic and the French and Belgium National Radio Orchestras. She has also performed with the Israel Philharmonic, the Osaka Philharmonic and the Hong Kong Philharmonic and has worked with such well-known conductors as Sir Andrew Davis, Charles Dutoit, Hans Graf, Bernard Haitink, Kyril Kondrashin, Lorin Maazel, Zubin Mehta, Sir Roger Norrington, Sir Georg Solti, Leonard Slatkin, Stanislaw Skrowaczewski and Klaus Tennstedt.

Janina Fialkowska was the founder of the "Piano Six" project and its successor "Piano Plus." The idea behind the latter initiative is to bring together some of

Canada's greatest classical artists (pianists, instrumentalists and vocalists) and Canadians who, for whatever reason, would not have an opportunity to hear the "live" classical performance. In 2000, the latter project was conspicuously recognized with the Chalmer's Award, one of Canada's top arts' awards.

"I've lost count of how many performances of Chopin's two piano concerti I've heard live and on disc in the last 12 months. Most have done this beautiful music full justice—none more than Janina Fialkowska's breathtaking period-piano outing with Tafelmusik," wrote John Terauds in *The Toronto Star*.

Another Polish Canadian musical star is Andrzej Rozbicki. He came to Canada in 1985. Since then he has been a teacher at Toronto's Bishop Marrocco/Thomas Merton High School and has achieved success working with several choirs in Canada. For five years he conducted the Brampton Symphony Orchestra, an ensemble he organized. He currently works with a newly created choir, the Polonia Singers, and with the Celebrity Symphony Orchestra.

In 1999, Rozbicki was awarded the Senate of Canada Award of Merit, and in 2000 he was given the Mayor's Toronto Millenium Award. In March 2006 he was awarded the Knight's Order of Polonia Restituta by the president of the Republic of Poland and a Gold Honorary Award by the Canadian Polish Congress. In May 2006 he received the University of Toronto Outstanding Associate Teacher Award 2005–2006—Ontario Institute for Studies in Education (OISE).

Creating a symphony orchestra practically from scratch sounds like an impossible task. It is, however, an important enterprise in a society flooded with mechanical and commercial music. The Celebrity Symphony Orchestra (CSO) is not only a group of entertainers—as Toronto councillor Peter Milczyn said, "Each concert of Celebrity Symphony Orchestra is a feast for the soul. It is really important to popularize the achievements of Polish art and culture on Canadian scene; it determines to a large extent our image here."

One Polish Canadian symphony orchestra would be a considerable contribution of Polish immigrants to Canadian culture. In fact, however, there are two.

Toronto Sinfonietta came to being in 1986. Its music director, Matthew Jaśkiewicz, together with his Polish friends of musical interests, founded a group called the Polish Canadian Society of Music. The group quickly grew to two ensembles of musicians devoted to playing the early music of the Ars Antiqua Chamber Orchestra and Ars Antiqua Choir. Gradually, the orchestra expanded its repertoire. The name of the group was changed to Musica Antiqua, and finally, in 1990, to Toronto Sinfonietta.

The next stage of development of the ensemble and the next step in its career on the Toronto musical scene was establishing a partnership with Oakham House Choir of the Ryerson University. The concerts were moved to the Glenn Gould Studio in the Canadian Broadcasting Centre in downtown Toronto. The growing popularity of the ensemble allowed the musicians of Toronto Sinfonietta and the Choir to expand their repertoire and include a rich collection of magnificent oratorios, including Handel's "Messiah" and Orff's "Carmina Burana."

The ensemble, under the direction of Jaśkiewicz, then ventured into the realm of opera. Beginning with concert arias, the Toronto Sinfonietta presented full-scale operas, starting with better-known compositions such as "Orpheus and Euridice" by Christoph Gluck and "Idomeneo" by Wolfgang Amadeus Mozart. In 1996 the ensemble gave the Canadian public the opportunity to become acquainted with a lesser-known work: a full production of "Halka," an opera by a Polish Romantic composer named Stanisław Moniuszko. Subsequently, Polish music played an increasing role in building the repertoire of the Toronto Sinfonietta. Assisted by other Polish Canadian music ensembles active in Ontario—the Polish Symfonia choir and other Polish choirs from Toronto and Hamilton—Toronto Sinfonietta staged two major performances of Polish music: Karol Kurpiński's religious oratorio "Te Deum" and Wojciech Kilar's composition "Angelus," popularized when it was used in the motion picture *City of Angels*, starring Nicholas Cage and Meg Ryan.

Toronto Sinfonietta constantly bears in mind that it is a Canadian ensemble and should cultivate Canadian repertoire. Thus, for the 1998–99 season, composer Ronald Royer became the ensemble's composer-in-residence. Royer is one of the best-known contemporary Canadian composers and his works have been presented to audiences all over Canada, the U.S., as well as in Finland, Greece, Czech Republic and Germany. The cooperation of the composer with the orchestra brought about their most significant, so far, artistic realization: the recording of the *Romancing Chopin* CD. The collection provides the listener with original, creative arrangements of the composer's music, supplemented by original compositions by Ronald Royer and Alexander Rapoport. The Canadian artists were motivated for these compositions by the music of the great Romantic Polish composer.

Matthew Jaśkiewicz constantly searches for new musical challenges and new avenues to explore. The latest initiative by Toronto Sinfonietta is to venture into more popular genres of symphonic pop music and musical humour. In the 2010–11 season, the Toronto Sinfonietta charmed its listeners with a concert presenting the lighter side of Mozart's music, and they are working on an original arrangement of traditional English Christmas Carols that is sure to delight audiences.

Polish Canadian music achievements have a bright future. Janina Fialkowska is an accomplished artist of world reputation, and CSO and Toronto Sinfonietta are well-established ensembles with significant achievements. In Calgary, however, a new talent of impressive scale is growing up from Polish roots on fertile Canadian soil. Jan Lisiecki was born in Calgary to Polish immigrant parents in 1995. He began studying music at the age of five at Mount Royal University Conservatory. He states:

I concisely remember the moment when my hands and feet gradually gained control and I was able to make the piano sing. My powerful relationship with the piano began and I started to discover my voice. As I play, I feel that the magic of the music is emerging from the piano, and also is developing in me—I feel the light shining into my heart. I experience joy, happiness, love; but also sadness and pain. And I have the strong desire to share it with others.

Still a teenager, Jan can boast of impressive achievements. Since his orchestral debut at the age of nine, he has performed more than 50 times with orchestras in Canada and internationally, including the National Arts Centre Orchestra, Montréal Symphony Orchestra, L'Orchestre Symphonique de Québec, Sinfonietta Cracovia, Minnesota Orchestra, Suwon Philharmonic Orchestra, and Sinfonia Varsovia, to name a few.

On January 1, 2010, Jan opened the celebrations for Chopin's 200th birthday from the composer's birthplace, in Żelazowa Wola. In the same month, Jan gave a "dazzling" performance of the "Chopin Concerto No. 1 in E minor" at the MIDEM Classical Awards Gala in Cannes, France. In July 2010 he performed for Her Majesty the Queen of England and 100,000 people on Parliament Hill in Ottawa. In October of the same year he signed an exclusive contract with Deutsche Grammophon.

Jan has played at Carnegie Hall, the Warsaw Philharmonic Concert Hall, Kaufman Hall, Salle Cortot and has shared the stage with Yo-Yo Ma, Pinchas Zukerman, James Ehnes and Emanuel Ax. He has performed in the United States, Korea, China, Japan, France, Germany, England, Scotland, Italy, Guatemala, Poland and throughout Canada.

He performs frequently for various charity organizations, including the David Foster Foundation, the Polish Humanitarian Organization and the Wish Upon a Star Foundation. In June 2008 he was appointed a National Youth Representative by UNICEF Canada.

Moving from the music scene to the literary, from 1985 to 1988 I worked for Radio Canada International, a Polish language shortwave radio program, in Montréal. My colleague there was Ewa Stachniak, also a recent immigrant from Poland. We wrote and produced programs about Canada, until the CBC administration decided that the enterprise cost too much and closed the broadcast. I went on to work in Washington, and Ewa moved to Toronto to teach English at Sheridan College—and to write in English, her second language.

Ewa's first short story, "Marble Heroes," was published in 1994 by *The Antigonish Review*. Her first novel, *Necessary Lies*, won the Amazon.com/Books in Canada First Novel Award in 2000. Her second novel, *Garden of Venus*, has been published in Canada, the UK, Australia, New Zealand, Greece, Spain, Italy, Brazil, Serbia, Poland and Ukraine. The third novel, *The Winter Palace*, is forthcoming.

Her work is highly praised by top reviewers: "Stachniak writes with brief, often poetic sentences, managing to create a rich sense of place and period through evocative details. In a novel that continually returns to the image of the garden, both lush and rotting, both good and evil, it seems fitting that bodily functions— sex, birth, death—are presented in dual images of horror and bliss." (Caroline Skelton, *Quill & Quire*) "Historical fiction of the very best kind." (*Edmonton Journal*)

Polish Canadians are involved in Canadian music and literature, in fine art, the media and architecture.

They are also, for example, present in the world of photography. Andrew Stawicki learned photography in Poland and brought his skills to Canada in 1982, joining the staff of *The Toronto Star*. His photographs appeared in *A Day in the Life of...* books on Canada, Japan, the U.S., Spain and the Soviet Union; he is a gold medallist in the Society of Newspaper Design awards and Canadian Association of Professional Image Creators awards. He twice won the National Newspaper Award and published a book, *People Apart*, the result of his 10-year study of the Mennonites.

Stawicki was also one of the founders of a unique artistic enterprise in Canadian media art, called Photo-Sensitive. These talented artists work in black-and-white photography. Although a somewhat outmoded medium, this kind of presentation not only jolts the audience with the help of unexpected imagery, but it also serves to deepen the understanding of significant social issues by the Canadian audience.

On the other side of the vast land of Canada resides Andrzej Kiełbowicz. Also an experienced staff photographer from Poland with publications in major magazines in the country, he decided to come to Canada and investigate with his camera the scenic land and its fascinating people. He still photographs, but his major interest now is teaching digital photography to others.

> In the last six years I have renewed my interest in photography due to the amazing new possibilities brought on by the digital revolution. Stunned by the spectacular revival of photography, I decided to share with my students my broad working knowledge of

professional photography, visual arts, graphic design, and related computer technology.

Andrzej's contribution to the Canadian photographic scene may not be large, but there are many Canadians who gain satisfaction from taking snapshots or artistic photographs with their digital equipment, thanks to Andrzej Kiełbowicz.

POLISH CANADIANS IN SPORTS

Art is important to every society, but Canada is first of all a hockey country. Wayne Gretzky may be of mixed Polish or Byelorussian descent, but Wojtek Wolski is definitely Polish. He was drafted into the NHL in 2004 by the Colorado Avalanche on the basis of his unprecedented four-in-a-row Ontario Hockey League Player of the Month awards and an MVP title for 2006. After getting six points in the last nine games of the regular season, he debuted for the Avalanche in the 2005¬–06 playoffs, recording a sensational three points in the first game against the Dallas Stars on April 22, 2006.

Traded to the Phoenix Coyotes in 2010, Wolski took revenge on his former team, scoring a game-winning goal against the Colorado Avalanche with 22 seconds left in the third period. In the 2010–11 season, he was traded again, this time to New York Rangers, but he "failed to click" with his new team. Fortunately, he is only 25, and there is still hope that he may become the "Polish Rocket" of the NHL. A commentator on the HockeyWriters website wrote an article on Wojtek entitled "Overlooked and Underrated."

Hockey aside, Canada is not closed to other sport disciplines. The choices are becoming wider, and Polish immigrants have contributed to this variety in a meaningful way, for example, by introducing some sports and providing experienced coaching staff.

One sport that, regretfully, rarely finds its way to the first pages of sport magazines is rhythmic gymnastics. It is a photogenic, women-only discipline traditionally popular in Eastern and Central Europe. "Traditionally," because this elegant sport is gaining popularity, and countries from all over the world were represented at the 2010 world championships.

In Canada, rhythmic gymnastics clubs exist and gain popularity in almost all provinces. The sport is particularly popular in British Columbia and Québec, where the 2011 World Cup tournament took place. The first Olympic Games to feature rhythmic gymnastics were held in 1984 in Los Angeles, with Canadian Lori Fung being the first gymnast in the history of the discipline to take an Olympic title.

Building on that success, new clubs appeared on the scene utilizing the talents of among others, immigrants. One of the most popular and effective clubs, which can justly say with pride that it brought a new quality to the sport in Canada, is the Etobicoke Olympium Rhythmic Gymnastics club coached since 1986 by Danuta Śmiechowska and Małgorzata Wichrowska.

Etobicoke is the home of Erika-Leigh Stirton, 1998 Commonwealth Games champion and five-time national champion. Currently, Stirton occupies 12th position in world rhythmic gymnast ranking—the highest ever attained by a Canadian gymnast. The club history consistently boasts of national team members at the novice, junior and senior levels, as well as provincial champions. In addition, its national junior group champions won the gold medal at the 1997 Junior Pan American Games.

As one of the coaches told me, it was really just bad luck that the club could not be proud of a medal won at the Sydney Olympics; its best competitor, Stirton, had excellent chances to come back from Sydney with an Olympic medal. Unfortunately, shortly before the Games she injured her foot playing school soccer. The club is working toward finding and preparing the next champion. It may be a young Polish Canadian named Joanna Matkowska, who is apparently bestowed with great talent for the sport, as confirmed by her three titles as Canadian champion.

In the meantime, the coaches do all they can to popularize the sport, stressing its value for general physical development of young women, the elegance it instils in their posture and movement and teaching the true value of sportsmanship. After all, rhythmic gymnastics is beyond doubt an amateur (not amateurish!) competition. Because of financial constraints, the Canadian gymnastics association provides national track suits to competitors; other expenses (transportation, hotels, meals and other expenses connected with participating in competitions) have to be covered by the gymnast or her family.

Still, the coaches and athletes work tirelessly at expanding the possibilities of physical education of Canadian youth. And not only in Toronto; another powerhouse in this sport is the Alegria program offered in Winnipeg since 2004 (also thanks to cooperation with Polish Gymnastic Association "Sokół", active in Winnipeg since 1906!). The head coach there is Natalia Rybak from Russia, who also spent many years coaching in Poland.

From banking to fine art, from music to literature, from hockey to gymnastics—the roughly 80,000 Polish immigrants who came to Canada in the 1980s and 1990s made a significant contribution to the life of the country. They enriched the Canadian ethnic fabric with specifically Polish qualities (like the taste for perogies), but they also demonstrated ability and readiness to excel in areas traditionally established in Canada.

Integration for Polish Canadians happened quickly, and, in most cases, was an easy process. And Canada is richer for their contributions.

I would recommend trying some traditional Polish food products and cuisine available in Starsky in Mississauga, but I would also gladly invite you to a Polish-organized festival of sea shanties, which for the last five years has attracted a growing number of admirers, many of whom do not even speak Polish.

CHAPTER NINE

ALL OVER THE COUNTRY

At the beginning of this book, I stated that Polish footprints can be found in the most unexpected places in Canada. However, for decades, since at least the end of World War II, the centre of Polish settlement in Canada has mostly been in the Greater Toronto Area. Barring the settlers who were dumped from the trains in Winnipeg, or moved slightly farther west to Saskatchewan and Alberta, most Polish immigrants arrived at the GTA and stayed there. Most, but not all, and the time has come to trace, at least roughly, some of the tracks left in other nooks and crannies of this vast land. The list is far from complete; a detailed history of Polish arrivals to Canada still awaits an author. The reader who has arrived at this point of the narrative deserves, however, an explanation how a remote bay in the Canadian arctic got the name

Strzelecki Harbour, named after a geologist who never visited Canada.

Paweł Strzelecki earned his fame in Australia. His work there received praise and recognition, and he also became one of the prominent members of the scientific elite in London. Strzelecki was made a Fellow of the Royal Geographical Society and awarded a gold medal for "exploration in the south eastern portion of Australia." The society still displays his huge geological map of New South Wales and Tasmania for public viewing. He was also made a member of the Royal Society and gained widespread recognition as an explorer as well as a philanthropist.

It was through this character of philanthropy that he contributed handsomely to the cost of equipping another expedition to search for the British explorer Sir John Franklin lost in his pursuit of the elusive North-West Passage. The command of the expedition was given to Francis McClintock. The expedition, as we know from Canadian history, did not find Sir John Franklin or his crew, but it did make some important discoveries in the Arctic. One of the islands discovered and charted by McClintock was named Prince of Wales Island. One of the geographical features of the land was named, as was the custom in those days, after a generous contributor to the cost of the expedition, Sir Paweł Strzelecki. Strzelecki Harbour is probably the only Polish geographical name in the arctic wasteland of North America. Let us, then, leave it at that and search other regions of Canada.

Soon after Newfoundland won the right to Representative Government, in 1832, it became apparent that one of the first challenges facing the new government would be to find an adequate place to house its Legislature. The cornerstone of the Colonial Building was laid on Queen Victoria's birthday, May 24, 1847. The building's completion was delayed by various minor incidents, and it welcomed its first visitors two years and 28 days later than it was originally scheduled. The Colonial Building is a spectacular example of fine architecture. The ceilings of the building are of particular interest. They were painted in 1880 by a Polish fresco painter named Alexander Pindikowski. Mr. Pindikowski had come to Newfoundland to teach art in the small village of Heart's Content. However, he gained fame in Newfoundland history through his arrest for attempting to cash forged cheques, and not for his artistic or pedagogical achievements.

On March 10, 1880, Pindikowski was arrested in St. John's. He was convicted of forgery and received a sentence of 15 months in prison. The government, however, realized the opportunity and recognized Pindikowski's talents as a fresco painter. He was put to work during the day on the ceilings of the Council Chamber and the Assembly Room at the Colonial Building. Pindikowski's hard work and the talent he exhibited was also recognized—his sentence was shortened by one month.

Proceeding east from Newfoundland, in Nova Scotia, there is a vibrant, if not large, Polish community in Halifax. They have their ethnic stores and even two folk dance ensembles. For some reason, however, the city became a favourite of Polish artists of the region. A group of painters, photographers and sculptors recently formed a Nova Scotia Society of Polish Artists under the directorship of Wanda Szubielski, painter and architect. The society is a relatively new initiative, but its first exhibition in October and November 2008 at Pier 21 gallery was well received by the local critics.

The exhibit included wood-carving and precise pencil drawings by religious wood sculptor Paweł Dumka; Zofia Aue's crisp, enigmatic figurative paintings and softer, still-life pastels; a huge, joyful hooked rug called Jazzorama by Amherst family doctor Halina Bieńkowski; textile art by Teresa Machel; and Szubielski's abstracts that are dramatic, disrupted architectural landscapes describing states of being.

The group's variety of imagery and styles is the "beauty of it," said Zibby Kwiatek, who came to Halifax in 1989 and works as a welder at the Halifax Shipyard. He started *The Marine Worker* for the Canadian Auto Workers/Marine Workers Federation. Kwiatek believes Nova Scotia is "paradise" for a photographer and does his best to prove it with his works.

If you're in the area and looking for a different kind of cuisine, the Halifax website (www.thecoast.ca) suggests Jannina's Café in Dartmouth. Melissa Buoter entitled her review of the café "Polish Delight" and stated:

> It's not a restaurant with a storied mythology or a celebrity chef. It's not in a popular neighbourhood or on a convenient nearby corner. It, like dozens of other tiny mom-and-pop places that pepper the city, anonymous and unheralded, is just a small storefront with a take-out counter, a handful of tables and regular customers who perhaps look at it as their happy little secret.... I still don't know if my answer to, "Hey, where

do you want to have lunch?" is going to be "Burnside," but if I'm in that neighbourhood, there's a good chance I'll say "Jannina's."

If, on the other hand, you tend to rely on official sources, please do not bypass an entry by Heritage Division, NS Department of Tourism under the title of St. Mary's Polish Church in Whitney Pier, Nova Scotia. The church was built of wood in Gothic style between 1913 and 1918. It has a 20-metre-high spire. St. Mary's Polish Church has played an important role in maintaining the multicultural heritage of Nova Scotia, and its history ties in with the process of the industrialization of the province.

Polish immigrants in Sydney began organizing their own place of worship by creating a St. Michael's Benefit Society in 1909. The institution served its members by providing disability insurance for those employed at the Sydney Steel Plant. Its second aim was to establish a social and religious base for the Polish community. In 1911, the Polish community of Sydney asked the Diocese of Antigonish for a Polish priest. Reverend Antoni Pluciński was sent to work with the community. Two years later, the society purchased four lots of land to build a church and glebe house. By September 1913 the church basement was completed and consecrated by Bishop Morrison of Antigonish.

For about four years, Mass was celebrated in the basement of the church until the congregation raised enough money to complete the building. That was achieved in 1918, largely through the dedication, volunteer labour and generous donations of the Polish community. St. Mary's Polish Church is the only church east of Montréal that serves a Polish Canadian community.

Speaking of Montréal, it is at present the second most important Polish community in Canada. In a way, though, it may be considered more important than the GTA. Since World War II, the city has been the centre of Polish scientific initiatives in Canada. In 1943 a group of Polish academics who found refuge in Montréal, together with a number of their Canadian colleagues and with the enthusiastic support of the eminent Polish historian Professor Oskar Halecki, then at Columbia University, founded the Canadian section of the Polish Institute of Arts and Sciences in America. Subsequently the Canadian section became the Polish Institute of Arts and Sciences in Canada with branches in Ottawa, Toronto and Vancouver. The founders' two major goals for the new institution were to preserve cultural and intellectual values threatened in Poland by the war and its geopolitical consequences and to acquaint Canadians with Polish history and culture.

With the defeat of the Communist regime, Poland regained its independence. Its culture is thriving and is no longer endangered from the outside. The institute is thus able to focus its activities on promoting Polish culture in Canada, reinforcing Polish Canadian friendship and serving the cultural needs of the Polish Canadian communities. The institute organizes lectures and meetings that are open to all members of the scientific community, and it supports publications of scientific and popular nature. But first of all, it takes care of the Polish Library at McGill University, presently named after Wanda Stachiewicz, its director, the wife of Polish chief of staff in 1939, General Wacław Stachiewicz.

Hard work and perseverance complemented Wanda's love of culture and the arts. It bore fruit in the creation of the institute. The primary means of achieving its goals were lectures, art exhibits and literary contests. Wanda Stachiewicz also gave a series of lectures on the history of Polish culture, and in 1973 she wrote a book titled *Copernicus and the Changing World* to celebrate the 500th anniversary of the astronomer's birth.

In 1946, Wanda was instrumental in the founding of the Polish Library and worked as its director for over 40 years. Even her retirement did not diminish her interest in the library. In 1984 the library was renamed The Wanda Stachiewicz Polish Library, to underscore her work and enthusiasm.

In recognition of her outstanding contributions to the Polish community in Canada, Wanda was awarded the gold medal of the Canadian-Polish Congress. And yet for all her accomplishments, Wanda's greatest joys and pride came from the love of her family and their successes and accomplishments.

"I have seen the old world die and a new world emerge. I never retired. The newness and the changes fascinate me. I am always ready to learn," said Wanda. It was this spirit of the love of knowledge and openness to new ideas that enabled Wanda to play so many roles in her life: author, scholar, lecturer, community activist and library director. The library offers its guests a choice of over 50,000 volumes of books and countless newspapers, magazines, maps, VHS cassettes, CDs and DVDs in Polish, English and French. The library's catalogue is integrated with that of McGill University. Thus, it is the only Polish-language library collection integrated with the library collection of a North American university.

On a more sombre note, in Pointe Claire near Montréal, there is a unique cemetery called "Field of Honour." Its uniqueness came from the fact that it is the only cemetery in Canada where only veterans of the armed forces are buried. Of more than 12,000 graves, 339 of them mark the burial sites of Polish soldiers from 1932 to 2003.

Another group of Polish graves are found in a little cemetery in Saint-Sauveur-des-Monts in the Laurentides. The Polish sector of the cemetery is the resting place of many prominent members of the Polish community in Montréal, including the graves of General Antoni Szylling, the commander of Polish Army "Kraków" in the September Campaign of 1939; the minister of foreign affairs of the Polish Government in Exile, Tadeusz Romer; the last Consul General of Poland to Canada before 1939, father of the American statesman, Tadeusz Brzeziński; and Vice-Admiral Stefan Frankowski, one of the builders of the Polish navy.

You may think that the smallest Canadian province, Prince Edward Island, is too tiny to house anything Polish. But you would be wrong. If you wish to spend some of your summer near the house of Anne of Green Gables, a good choice is the White Sands Resort in North Rustico. Krzysztof Opyto and his family vacationed there in 2006 and fell in love with the island. Opyto and his wife decided to check on the availability of businesses for sale. White Sands was the first one they visited, and their search stopped there. Today, the resort welcomes campers and families looking for cottages to rent, offers bus rides to the beach half a kilometre away and to all the attractions connected with Anne of Green Gables and Lucy Maud Montgomery centred around North Rustico. As an additional attraction, the owner of the resort is a fully qualified scuba diver, so guests can safely experiment with that sport in the waters around the island.

After a rest on PEI, it may be of interest to trace the footprints of hardworking Polish Canadians in Hamilton, Ontario. The first Polish settlers probably arrived here in the 1890s. These dozen or so immigrants possibly came from the United States, but nothing else is known about them. The first known Polish family in Hamilton was that of Frank and Anna Bielakowicz. Polish population of Hamilton grew with the establishment of the International Harvester Company (which started as Dering's Implements), and which employed Polish workers.

Reliable, honest, hardworking Poles were an asset to the new firms, and the companies often went out of their way to attract them. Dering's Implements made an attempt to help the Polish immigrants build their own church, but those plans unfortunately were not successful.

The second Polish immigration wave to Hamilton occurred around 1911. Immigrants of the second wave remained in Canada permanently. The community did not have its own church, but Mass was celebrated by Anglo-Saxon German priests in St. Ann's Catholic Church. Finally, in December 1911, the Hamilton diocese granted permission for the construction of the first Polish church, St. Stanislaus Church.

The first Polish pastor, Reverend Thomas Tarasiuk, came to Hamilton from Kitchener. It took just over a year to build a church at a cost of $30,000. The building is relatively large and ornately decorated. One can only wonder how such a small and impoverished community could afford the construction. Father Tarasiuk was instrumental in bringing the project to fruition and was similar in many ways to early Scottish, English and Irish churchmen who took care of the spiritual needs of the first Canadian settlers. He understood that the survival of the community depended on its spiritual and moral well-being. He had to build God's house from nothing, often against tremendous odds. And he conquered all the complications involved in such a project, including shortage of support and lack of money.

One of the first Polish businesses in Hamilton was general store on Gerrard Street started by Joseph and Maria Stemski. The general store became later a confectionery store and then a butcher shop, before it was sold by the descendants of the original owners. By that time, Hamilton had acquired a Polish cinema, a dairy company, a hotel and other businesses.

In 1928, Hamilton's Polish businessmen established their own organization, the Association of Polish Businessmen and Manufacturers. Its statutory goal was to promote trade between Canada and Poland and to help develop local Polish-owned businesses. The association is credited with stimulating the creation of similar businessmen's groups in other cities and with eventually improving the economic situation of Poles in Canada. Since 1932, the Polish-Hamiltonian Citizens Club has helped its members obtain Canadian citizenship and offers general assistance according to their needs. The club formed the Polish singing club called Hejnał (established in 1936 by S. Dudzic, W. Dubiel, S. Mazur and J.K. Flis), the Association of the Polish Youth Club at the Polish parish and the Polish Youth Club of Juliusz Słowacki, with the goals of assisting young people and the promotion of culture and sports. Today, Hamilton and its steelworks still attract many Polish Canadians.

London and Lakehead, Ottawa and Wawa, Sydney in Nova Scotia and Victoria in BC—the list of Polish footprints is long. And whatever the efforts of this author, the list will always be incomplete. According to the data from 2006 national census, almost 48,000 Polish Canadians live in Calgary, Alberta. Calgary Poles have their own radio and TV stations.

According to Canada's 1996 census, Yukon Territory had only 30,766 inhabitants. Of these, 625 declared Polish as their ethnic origin. Recently, Marcin Gienieczko, Polish journalist and travel writer, visited Yukon Territory. He is probably one of the most travelled journalists from Poland who specializes in feats of unparalleled daring. One of his former journeys was to walk along the Pyrenees Mountains on the border between France and Spain. Most people consider it an achievement to cross a mountain range; Gienieczko walked along the mountain range, from the Mediterranean to the Atlantic. Visiting the Yukon Territory, he decided to conquer two dangerous white-water trails, down the Yukon River in an inflatable pontoon and down the Mackenzie in a 12-foot (3.6-metre) canoe.

Traces of Polish presence can be seen everywhere. Even in the farthest arctic regions. Hardly a newspaper in Canada noticed and informed its readers about the spectacular achievement of a Polish Canadian runner, living presently in New York—Alicja Barahona. She is a world-renowned ultra-marathon runner and has run across the Sahara Desert. Looking for a different kind of wilderness, she decided to run from Inuvik to Tuktoyaktuk, a distance of 370 kilometres across probably the harshest conditions a runner can find in the world. On April 10, 2011, at approximately 3:50 PM, she ran into Tuktoyaktuk accompanied over the last 30 kilometres by the members of the Inuvik Run Club and was cheered on by residents of the community and the local RCMP.

"It was truly an Arctic Challenge. I had at least three times where I questioned how I was going to make it. I almost became one with the ice road as I was battling the bitter conditions that I was faced with. The wind was high and it was below minus 40 degrees Celsius," Barahona noted in her Internet blog. "This run was about helping raise awareness and funds for the Inuvik Homeless Shelter, and so far we have approximately $20,000 and counting."

It is said that footprints remain in the arctic snow for centuries. It is hoped that evidence of Barahona's impressive feat will remain along the Inuvik–Tuktoyaktuk route for a long time to come.

CHAPTER TEN

THREE PERSONAL STORIES OF POLISH CANADIANS

istory is not a record of facts and figures. As the word implies, it is a record of stories. And stories are usually full of characters—interesting or boring, notable or insignificant. However, they are the focal point of a story and of history. This is particularly true of Canadian history. Our country's history is still relatively fresh, its figures usually too large to comprehend. How do you visualize, for instance, over 240,000 kilometres of Canadian coastline? A person walking at the speed of five kilometres per hour, eight hours per day, would need almost 14 years to cover that distance. So Canadian history is the story of people who came to these shores and of those who welcomed them. Following are the stories of three randomly chosen Polish Canadians who settled in Canada in the last quarter century. The interviews were conducted in 2011 in Mississauga.

Leszek Dziadecki

Q: Where in Poland did you come from?

I come from Bieszczady, a remote area in southeastern Poland. I was born in Sanok, I grew up there, completed my education to high school level. It is a very nice place. But I had to leave Sanok to complete my education. I chose the Warsaw Polytechnic, department of automotive engineering. It proved to be something completely different from what I do today. At that time it was an interesting place to study. I started my university education in 1981, so my first year included strikes and all other events of the Solidarity period. It was truly fascinating. I believe that those were the times when it really was interesting to do university studies at that time, regardless of the university. It was truly educational, not just a rat race as now, whether here or there.

Q: Do you think you could briefly outline in one sentence your motives for leaving Poland?

The answer to this question should surprise you. We, Ewa [Leszek's wife] and I, lived a comfortable life in Poland. We had very loving families, so in fact our idea was to go abroad for summer holidays, for a limited time, to travel, maybe earn some cash. A year earlier we visited Italy, where a lot of people stayed and went to refugee camps. We came back to Poland after our summer holidays to complete another year at the university. So we went to the U.S. feeling this is the last opportunity before completing our education and further stabilization. So, we went for summer holidays, which somehow got slightly extended.

There was no premeditated possibility of emigrating. We searched around for a place we would like. We did not like Chicago, our original destination, so we ended up in New York, among some university friends. We extended our stay there, felt more or less at home, and so it somehow turned from summer holidays to permanent residence.

Q: And from New York you came to Canada; do you remember your first impressions of this country?

After living in New York City for four years, we loved Canada: its empty spaces, its beautiful architecture, its vistas. We came to Mississauga, and the city centre at that time, in 1991, was something completely different from today. Mississauga was green, full of space and studded with beautiful, single, spacious buildings. It was a charming city in the process of being born. You have to remember also that New York City then was different than it is now. It was dirty, devastated, smeared with graffiti, dangerous. So Canada was great, until the moment when we decided to settle here. We were self-sponsored immigrants, with some cash to our names. Canada was beautiful, until we had to start looking for work. Please remember: we are talking of 1991, the time of depression, and no offers on the labour market. Even a decent apartment was difficult to find. We were a little disappointed. The country seemed wonderful, but we came here with five years of U.S. experience, where we did interesting work in relatively high positions. We expected to come here and be greeted with open arms, and all of a sudden we found out that we have "no Canadian experience." Everything else was practically useless. On the other hand, when we tried to find work at a lower level, we were told that we were overqualified and no one wanted to risk employing us, because we may one day leave for something better. The situation was unpleasantly paradoxical, but we have to remember that we came here almost exactly at the time of a serious economic depression in Canada.

Q: So, you decided to change your professions?

I have practically never entered my university profession, as you can imagine. The automotive industry in North America is something completely different than in Poland of the 1980s. During my stay in New York I caught the bug of organizing and running a business. I helped a man in New York to do it in his name, and I was hoping I could find a similar position here in Canada. I searched around, tried almost everything, including multilevel marketing. I tried to find my way around in a new scenery. I also had another reason to change my profession. We brought some savings from the U.S. and we wanted to invest that money. I went to see a broker, followed his advice and invested the money. A few months later there was nothing left. The broker was not at fault; it was the market. The companies we invested in disappeared. I was understandably very frustrated, but I met a man who worked in the field, I became interested in finances, started learning new things, completed the necessary courses, got my designations and licences, and promised myself that no one ever will play with our money again.

Q: It was also a family reunion of sorts?

Yes, my father was a bank manager in Sanok. I grew up in an apartment over the bank. He was very happy to learn that I ended up following in his footsteps. There is more to it though: my father was fascinated by automobiles. Around 1970 there were three cars in Sanok, and one of them was the property of my father. So, in a way, I originally chose my career following his fascination with the motor industry, but finally ended up in his profession.

Q: After all these years, is your profession just a way of earning money, or is there something more to it?

If I cared for my money only, I would be doing it on my own, without the effort of building up a separate business. I created and I manage the Advantage Group of Finance because my experience tells me there is a need for this kind of service. There is a need for an honest broker, for a place where the clients can come to arrange loans, purchase insurance and so on. There is a need for financial advice and help. We started the business in the years when there were a lot of newcomers from Poland to Canada, and most of them had no idea whatsoever how these things work. Our education in Poland was excellent; we learned tons of things like history, geography. Polish people have wide general knowledge acquired in school, but have absolutely no inkling how the world of finances works and how it can be used to your advantage. We never learned the basics, except for those who chose finances or economics at the university, and even then it was mostly theory and much too little practice. There was a need, so we decided to try. Why not?

Q: Advantage Group of Finances started as a Polish community enterprise. Did you base your business on clients from our community?

Not really. That came later. We started the business, I don't really remember why, basing it on clients from the Philippines. That was about 60 to 80 percent of our clients. Only afterwards we expanded to the Polish market, the Russian one, the Canadian one, and so on.

Q: Many of the brokers working in Advantage Group of Finance are of Polish origin, but not all...?

Definitely not all. We have a Korean broker, a Vietnamese. It truly reflects the Canadian reality. Our people come from various corners of the world. We have a Chinese Canadian, Israeli Canadian—a really Canadian mix. There is, however, a definitely Polish atmosphere in our office. We like it and we found that even Canadians who came from other cultures find it appealing. They learn of our culture and appreciate it. The son-in-law of one of our brokers, a Korean Canadian, is a Polish Canadian.

Q: Would you say that your business contributes to building Canada?

I think so. And in more than one way. First of all, we really do help our clients. We help families save money, set it aside for later, for the education of their children. People come here with dreams, but reality can be much more difficult. We have been in the market for

17 years; there are clients of Advantage Group of Finance who educated their children thanks to the money they saved through our plans, with our help. They realize, and tell us so, that they would never have been able to do it were it not for our advice and help. So, in a small way, we contribute to the education of new Canadians. Another side of the business is insurance policies. People get older, get sick, and they need help. Thanks to our solutions, at least some of them could get that financial assistance. They would survive with governmental help, but it is limited, and it is a financial burden for the state.

Indirectly, we also contribute to creating and developing Canada through creating jobs, through paying taxes and so on. There are so many new people here, so much need, that Canada truly benefits from our presence on the market. We help fill a clear and significant need. That is why we are active on the so-called ethnic market, so that we can offer and provide the help I was talking about.

Q: Canada has been called a lot of things: a land of immigrants, a land of opportunity. How would you describe the country? What tag would you attach to Canada?

To me it is a land of endless possibilities. Here, no one fences you in. If you have an idea, if you want to do something in your life, you will find that in Canada you can do it. Somewhere else four neighbours and two business rivals will conspire to set you back. In Canada, it is up to you. Canadians may not support your initiative, but at least they will not generally block it. Canada is a friendly country. I will never forget when in 1993 I was taking a professional course and my lecturer spoke with a beautiful British accent. I was enchanted and told him I wish I could speak so beautifully. He replied, to my great surprise, that his accent is an impediment in his business. Most of the clients are newcomers, and some of them feel intimidated by a person speaking such proper English.

AGATA CYBULA

Q: How did it happen that you immigrated to Canada?

I came here in 1989, one month after graduating from the university in Poland. It was a difficult time for everyone there; the shortages of everything were unimaginable. The store shelves were literally filled with vinegar and mustard only. I never got to work in my profession in Poland. Together with Tomek, my husband, we decided we had to leave and look for something better. Tomek had some experience from abroad and he suggested we leave. So all we waited for was graduation. Even though we had a three-year-old son we decided to try our luck elsewhere.

We managed to get passports and tourist visas to Canada. Tomek was here earlier, so there was no trouble, and we applied to be together with him. Still as tourists. We, who came here at the end of the 1980s, are the last wave of immigrants who arrived here practically with nothing beside a couple of suitcases and a university diploma in our pockets. We were allowed to stay as tourists for three months. So, I had to work really hard and could not afford to fail a single exam.

Q: How did you manage to get landed immigrant papers?

At that time, there was in force a special program for Polish immigrants negotiated by Canadian Polish Congress with the ministry of immigration. We travelled by bus to Detroit to sign necessary papers and on this basis received landed immigrant status.

Q: Did you have to wait long?

A few months. What is more—I found out I was pregnant again. It was nerve-racking, because I could not tell what will come first: landed immigrant papers and OHIP coverage, or the baby. We had no idea how we would pay for the hospital stay if the papers were delayed. But it all ended well, the permanent resident status arrived just ahead of my second son. At the same time, I attended courses in English. From Poland I had no command of the language, as I took German at school. I did try to learn something even before we left Poland, but it was practically nothing. Remember, I had to get my university diploma first. So my first Canadian experience was—learn English, have a baby and get a high TOEFL score so that I can continue my studies. That was tough.

Q: What were your first impressions of Canada?

Of Toronto. And they were not complimentary. We ended up in some apartment building in Etobicoke— grey, sad. Tomek's sister took us to Bloor West Village, to downtown, but I thought this is terrible. All I remember from those days is the impression that all the houses are small and poor, people live in apartments or flats over the store. I was truly astonished.

Where is this fantastic, prosperous Canada? I had very little experience of travelling around the world, of visiting other countries in the West, but I still thought this is some backwoods village, not the great city of Toronto. Even downtown did not look too well, with the industrial chimneystacks right next to the Gardiner Expressway and the heart of the city. What is more, we were really busy those first couple of years. I had to get my professional designation as soon as possible, so there was no time for tourist experience or even a night out on the town. We gradually did get to see a little more, meet some people and find out that not the entire city looks the same, but that was gradual.

Q: Did the Canadian authorities help you in any way?

On the contrary. It was a time of a rather difficult relationship between the Polish immigrants, particularly seeking work in the medical field, and the Canadian authorities. When I was picking up my permanent resident papers, I had to sign a special document promising that I will not engage in protests, strikes and so on. I met other people in the same field who never managed to get their Canadian papers even though they kept on trying for eight or ten years. Many got discouraged in the process. I, however, seem to have had sufficient motivation to do my thing. At the same time, when I did my work for the courses and exams, I realized that the difference between what I learned in Poland and the Canadian standards was enormous. I practically had to study dentistry from the beginning—and doing it most of the time at home, with two children to take care of. You have to remember that even someone who completes his studies here, in Canada, knows very little and only of the basic stuff. It is only in practice, with a diploma in your pocket, that the true learning begins.

Q: You and your husband opened your own clinic very quickly; wouldn't it have been better to work for someone else at first?

I did work for others at the beginning. The demand for my services was however very limited. I got some work here and there, but not enough. At that time the new Polish centre "Tatry" was being opened, an opportunity came, so we took advantage of it. I opened my clinic in 1995 in the same complex where it still is located. It took me four years to get my licence, another year to open my clinic, and so it goes till now.

Q: Your clinic is widely known in the community for the support you give to local cultural events, is it not?

It started as a marketing device, particularly in the Polish community. Quickly, however, we started enjoying it. Today, it is more of a charitable donation. My clinic does not really need it. I have a lot of fun meeting visiting artists, welcoming them in my home. It brings some new quality to my life besides taking care of people's dental health.

I still remember going shopping with one of the stars of Polish pop music, and it's a lot of fun. And it gives me satisfaction when I know that I can welcome these artists and celebrities in a manner they deserve. They travel around the world, they visit various places and it is not everywhere that they are taken care of on the same level of hospitality. They see it and they compare. It's nice to feel that they will recall Toronto with pleasure. It gives them a nicer impression of Canada and Polish Canadians.

Q: It looks like your clinic is first of all a part of the Polish community...?

Not only. It was built basing the enterprise on the Polish community in Mississauga. I owe the community a lot, but today it is simply a Canadian clinic. I employ almost 20 people, and not all of them are of Polish origin. The same with the patients; I have a lot of patients who have nothing to do with Poland and the Polish community. They probably comprise at least a third of my patients. It may have been more, but most of my patients are faithful to the clinic. I have treated some of them for years, even from the beginning 16 years ago.

Today, I take care of patients who are the children of my patients. One day I expect to treat a grandchild of one of my original patients. A few days ago one of the patients said to me that he has been coming here for 20 years, even though he is only 21. I checked his file, and in fact he has been my patient for over 16 years. I treat young people and remember their mothers.... It feels like we are all part of one great big family. That is the best part of my job. I know they could go to some other clinic, but they come to me. And if they marry, they bring their wives and husbands to me for treatment.

Q: You were successful?

I feel that my many years of hard work bore fruit. The clinic has a reputation as a good place to go to, so I suppose I was successful. Hard work, that's all.

Q: Is it time to retire?

Definitely not. I may sell the clinic, or hand it over to my son's girlfriend, who works in the same field. But I don't think about it. I still have too much satisfaction doing what I do. All the more so that there is so much new stuff in my profession.... I really enjoy this work and all the innovations. It is fun. It is work, but it is also my hobby. I love my work.

Q: Looking back to 1989, was it worth it to move from Poland to Canada?

Definitely yes. Canada is nice, safe; we can be at home here. I don't feel a stranger in a strange land. After all, there are probably about 10,000 patient files in my clinic. And I am close with many of them.

MAREK ZIMNY

Q: How did you find yourself in Canada? What was the motivation for leaving Poland?

I was born and grew up in Wrocław. My sister came to Canada earlier, in 1980, and I decided to go and see her, and at the same time improve my English. I spoke German well, so it seemed reasonable to get a good knowledge of another language. That was my reason for coming here in the first place. Back in Poland I was an owner of a small business, we produced ceramics, I had a few people working for me. I was very well educated at the Polytechnic University of Wrocław and that was the base for everything I am doing now. I came to Canada for a brief visit and had no idea I will be staying here. During my university studies I had the opportunity to visit Western Europe, so when the opportunity came to visit North America, I said: "Why not?" Earn some money, practice my English and come back. That was the plan.

Q: Do you remember your first impression of Canada?

You have to remember that I came here from California, where I spent over a year prior to coming here, so my first impression was: "How cold it is!" Springs are short, winters are long, and everything is very expensive. I knew Canada is a very good country to live in, but I had no idea it is world standard in my kind of business. I heard of its reputation as one of the best places to emigrate to, from other Polish people who came here earlier, but I had no idea why it is so.

Q: Did you have any problems immigrating?

No, Canada embraced me. I joined my family here. I received landed immigrant status, I found work and I realized I could hold a dignified position here— better than anywhere in Europe. I was ready to sweep the streets for a living, I was ready for that, but it proved I could use my education, I could apply my knowledge and skills to work.

When I was interviewed in the Canadian consulate in California, I was asked what I want to do here. I told them that I want to use my education and open a business—and that is exactly what happened.

Q: Canada is often called the "land of opportunity"—is that your impression too?

It is a land of opportunity for people with education, with drive, ready to work hard. It is a stable country. If you compare it with the United States—there you can see a lot of junk cars on a highway, alongside fantastic, expensive vehicles. In Canada everything is more toned down, "middle of the road." And that applies to Canadian economy, lifestyle, everything. And—everything is healthy, long term, and not critical.

Q: How did you build your business?

It takes a lot of time, effort and other ingredients to create a successful business. I always wanted to build machines, I always wanted to have my own business, and I was helped by my education. I had "drive"; I had good foundations, so all I needed was some local experience. Thus, in 1995, 10 years after leaving Poland, I was ready.

Q: What does your company, Promation, do?

"Promation" is a combination of two words: "professional" and "automation." That is what we do. We use our engineering knowledge to design and sell custom equipment in the field of robotics and tooling. I supply equipment to the automotive market and—for the last five years—to the nuclear industry. Promation is just one of the companies in a very wide market.

The company grew steadily from its inception and now has more than 150 customers across North America, including Toyota, Honda and Chrysler. We have a lot of competitors, so they would be very glad if I disappeared from the market, but the market is not as well as it was in the 1990s, so I have to leverage myself to keep the company running. My biggest competitors are already down; I so far am not, but I have to be careful. I have to think of some 70 or so people working for the company.

Q: How did you get into the nuclear sector?

That is different. Atomic Energy of Canada Limited contracted Promation's services to develop tooling and robotic solutions for the nuclear industry. There are few competitors. Getting there is easy. All you need is your basic knowledge of engineering. For my company, it was the engineering expertise which helped. But it takes a lot of stamina to succeed. Afterwards, it is certification, proof that you know nuclear quality programs, and that is it.

Q: I've heard it said that your company saved the Canadian nuclear industry by repairing the Chalk River reactor...?

That is an exaggeration. Though, in a way.... What happened was: the reactor needed repairs. Atomic Energy Commission was looking for a company able to design tools necessary for the job. We got the contract, designed the robot and fixed the problem. It was a challenging proposition, but we did it. That's all, business as usual.

Q: One of these days the company will be running smoothly, and you will be able to retire. What will you do?

In business it's called succession. Nobody lives forever. I have a succession plan ready, and I want to implement it in five years—depending on the market. The company will survive me. Promation is to be a brand name in the industry, and that takes a long time. We are only 15 years in the business, and we are still growing. In five years I am going to double the business, for sure. And if I do retire, I will stay in Canada. It is a very good country. I have a son, a budding scientist, who is, after all, Canadian. But first of all I do not want to retire mentally. I plan to be really active all my life.

Q: Are you now, after 15 years, at home in Canada?

I just wish we had milder winters.

Q: What is your passion outside business?

Racing motorcycles in enduro events. You have to keep mental development in balance with physical. That's my passion.

Q: And your dream?

I want to build a robotic highway—first an experimental track from Toronto to Oakville. Cars would drive on it at the speed of 200 kilometres per hour. The technology is there. All I need is a billion dollars investment.

The personal histories I have narrated above have been (as I mentioned) selected at random. The businesses started by Leszek, Agata and Marek thrive in Canada's economy and serve all Canadians. It is important to note that the three entrepreneurs started their companies to provide for themselves and their families; today, they employ other specialists, offer high-quality services to the general public while raising the standards in their sectors and contribute to the growth of the Canadian economy.

Twenty-seven years ago, as a new Canadian, I met a Polish woman in Toronto, to whom I shall refer here only by her first name, Stasia. She was one of the immigrants who arrived in Canada in the 1960s—in her case, as a post-war bride of one of the Polish Army veterans resettled to Canada after World War II.

The couple worked in some menial jobs, bought a little house in the Little Poland neighbourhood near Roncesvalles Avenue and lived there, renting rooms to new immigrants. Stasia worked at a clothing factory for over 20 years, buried her husband and carried on living her ordinary, uneventful life, always cheerful and friendly, full of good advice based on her Canadian experience.

She lived in "Little Poland," worked with Polish-speaking co-workers, shopped at Polish stores and banked with the Polish Parishes Credit Union. In a quarter of a century she never managed to learn English but for a few words. Her advice to me was to find a job in the community and forget about "conquering

Canada." Her mindset was dominant in the ethnic ghetto of "Little Poland" of the 1950s and 1960s. A lot has changed since then.

"Little Poland" is alive and well—in Toronto, Montréal, Ottawa, Edmonton, Winnipeg, Vancouver, Halifax and in other cities across Canada. Polish immigrants still can live, if they choose, within their ethnic ghetto, never learning English, never integrating into the Canadian society. They can, but they choose not to. There is no need to stay in their own ethnic community and rely on their countrymen for all the essentials of life in Canada. It does not make sense to most Polish Canadians. Canada is, partly, ours. We, together with the Irish, the French, the Scots and the Chinese, among others, built it.

Appendix I
Polish Organizations in Canada

It is often said that Polish people have a reputation for individualism and a healthy dislike of joining organizations, preferring individual freedom of action to the constraints of organizational discipline. That may be true in other circumstances, but in Canada, Polish organizations of various kinds appeared almost simultaneously with the large influx of immigrants at the beginning of the 20th century. We should remember that the wave of Polish immigrants at that time consisted mainly of uneducated farmers with little professional expertise and practically no knowledge of any language other than Polish. What is more, they came from a country that did not exist on the map, so they also felt alienated and deserted, fighting for their existence against fate and all others. Polish national sentiment never expired in their homeland, so they had no reason to agree to similar "treason" in their new conditions of life.

Polish immigrants to Canada in the early 1900s felt different and separate from those they encountered in the new land, so they exhibited a stronger tendency to stay together, help one another and survive through common effort in a land so different from what they were accustomed to. Thus, Polish organizations in Canada were born almost immediately with the arrival of Polish immigrants, first to the centre of this immigration wave, in Manitoba, and slightly later in Saskatchewan and Alberta, together with the Polish settlements appearing there.

There was also an additional mechanism that forced Polish immigrants to cooperate and help one another: the attitude of the established population to the new-comers from Eastern Europe. They were treated as "dirty Galicians," so it was clearly in their interest to oppose this mistreatment and prejudice by establishing self-help and self-defence mechanisms. The specific conditions of the Canadian West encouraged such initiatives: the administration of those vast lands was sparse and weak, and practically no established authority was in place to enforce the laws and regulations to protect the weak and needy. Lack of strong, universal Canadian administration forced immigrants (not only the Polish) to rely on their own resources for protection against mistreatment.

The second strong factor influencing the creation of Polish organizations in Canada was the need to protect their national culture and identity. As I have mentioned, Poland did not exist on the map till 1918, but the Poles never gave up their dreams of an independent country to call their own. The fundamental need, thus, was the protection of the national feeling, culture, language, history and traditions.

Both these factors combined with the third characteristic feature of the Polish people at that time (and presently)—their faith. Poland is a strongly Catholic nation, probably equally Catholic as Spain and Italy. The Catholic Church is all-present in the life of the society, and the Sunday Mass is an essential element of both social and individual life. The church and its teachings regulate the life of practically every Pole and of every Polish family or settlement.

These three factors determined the creation of Polish organizations in Canada. Wherever a group of Poles settled on the Prairies, the Church followed almost immediately—first in the form of occasional visits of travelling priests who celebrated Mass in private homes, but then very quickly in the form of establishing a primitive locale that served as a church, as a centre of all social activities, as an educational establishment or simply as a place for social gatherings and interaction.

The church became much more than just a place of worship, and the Polish Catholic community that concentrated around it developed various other organizational forms, depending on its needs and potential. Whether we look at this mechanism from a historical or strictly religious point of view, the unity of place is immaterial. It is more the result of economy of place than of an ideological encroachment of the Catholic hierarchy on the life of the community—even if you could find instances of a conflict between these two.

The modern Catholic Church in Canada owes its existence to the efforts of a little-known organization in Europe called the Missionary Oblates of Mary Immaculate (OMI). Established in 1816 to revive the church after the French Revolution, the order received instructions to help with the missionary work of the Catholic Church in several countries, with a particular accent on Western Canada. Most of this work concerned the Native population, but priests of the order served also as parish priests in the Prairies, and many of them do so to this day.

The OMI founded the University of Ottawa in 1848, then the College of Bytown. Since the University of Ottawa became publicly funded in 1965, Saint Paul University exists as a separate but federated institution with a pontifical charter to grant ecclesiastical degrees and a public charter, through the University of Ottawa, to grant civil degrees.

Polish members of OMI, the three brothers Kulawy, were the first to take care of the spiritual needs of Polish immigrants in Manitoba, Saskatchewan and Alberta. The brothers established the first Polish parish in Canada and built the first Polish church—the Roman Catholic Holy Ghost Church in Winnipeg. They visited Polish settlers in Saskatchewan and in Alberta, around Edmonton and Calgary, as well as the coal mining settlements in the Rockies. Their work was continued by other Polish priests of the OMI, notably Father Antoni Sylla, whose published memoirs are probably the best source of information on the Polish Catholic Church in Canada.

One hundred years later, there are 44 Polish parishes in Canada with almost 200 priests. And every parish includes a dozen or more organizations more or less closely related to its primary function, which all serve the community and anyone else who may be interested in its activity.

CANADIAN POLISH CONGRESS

The congress, usually referred to by its Polish-language acronym KPK (Kongres Polonii Kanadyjskiej), is the most important Polish Canadian organization and is active all over the country. It is an umbrella federation for over 240 smaller organizations. The statute of the KPK states: "The Canadian Polish Congress is a Canadian organization that represents our community's interests before the people and Government of Canada. The Canadian Polish Congress promotes awareness of and respect for Poland's history and heritage and the contribution of Poles to the culture of Canada and the world." It states also that in its activity, the KPK will respect the laws of Canada, be aware of the good of Canada, Polish Canadians and the Polish nation.

The congress came into being in 1944, although its roots may be seen in the Federation of Polish Societies in Canada, established in 1928 in what was then the most important centre of Polish Canadians, in Winnipeg. Both the congress and its parent organizations were established because Polish Canadians wanted someone to represent their concerns to the Canadian authorities and the Canadian people. The original statute of the organization from 1931 states clearly: "No organization whose intentions include sudden change of the existing social order of the world, by revolution, will be permitted to belong to the Federation."

The article allowed the federation to eliminate all organizations showing pro-Communist tendencies, whatever their name or declared aims. By 1933, 33 declarations of membership were received, with an additional 16 organizations joining the following year, for a total membership of 3391 individuals.

In September 1944, a convention of the federation in Toronto decided to establish a new organization on similar lines—the Canadian Polish Congress.

Besides political representation of the community in contacts with the Canadian authorities and the authorities in Poland, the congress extends its activity to care and help for Polish Canadians and their compatriots in Poland, in the form of its charitable foundation. The congress was instrumental in the creation of the Canadian Polish Millennium Fund. The fund was created to commemorate the millennial anniversary of Christianity in Poland observed in 1966. The goal of the congress is to promote Polish culture in Canada and to preserve the Polish language. The objectives include aiding and encouraging education among people of Polish origin and descent, establishing scholarships and fellowships for students, financing the publication of scientific and literary works relating to Polish history and culture, and supporting Polish schools, libraries, academic institutions, Polish Scouts and other Polish community youth organizations in Canada.

Many Polish Canadians from the latest wave of immigrants arriving in Canada after the Communist crackdown on the Solidarity Union owe a great debt to the Canadian Polish Congress. The organization earned such respect with the Canadian authorities that an understanding was established between the ministry of immigration and the congress, allowing for the organization of a special immigration program for Polish refugees. Thousands of Poles arriving in Canada were allowed to seek immigration status through Canadian consulates in Buffalo and Detroit, speeding up the process and facilitating their settlement.

St. Stanislaus–St. Casimir's Polish Parishes Credit Union

The most important organizational initiative of Polish Canadians is not an organization, but a bank.

The Polish Parishes Credit Union was founded on August 9, 1945, thanks to the efforts of Father S. Puchniak, OMI, pastor of St. Stanislaus Parish in Toronto and his assistant Father M. Smith, OMI. The second office was set up in 1958 at St. Casimir's Parish because the needs of the Polish community were growing and a new office was required in another parish populated mainly by Polish immigrants. The credit union's role was to help Polish immigrants who could not receive proper service and understanding at regular Canadian banks.

In the 1980s, the St. Stanislaus–St. Casimir's Credit Union merged with a few other Polish credit unions in Toronto, Kitchener, Hamilton, Windsor and Oshawa to become the major Polish banking and loan institution and the largest ethnic credit union in Canada. At present, the credit union underscores with pride that it is not only the largest Polish financial institution outside of Poland but also the largest parish-based credit union in the world, with 16 branch offices, close to 40,000 members and total assets of over $388 million. The credit union provides a full range of financial services to its individual and corporate members, in person, over the telephone as well as online.

POLISH ALLIANCE IN CANADA

Although the Canadian Polish Congress is the main and the most representative Polish Canadian organization, the oldest and probably the largest by member count is the Polish Alliance in Canada, organized in 1924 in Toronto as an association of minor self-help organizations all over the country. The aims of the alliance are somewhat limited to activity in culture, education and publishing. Today, it is active first of all in Ontario. Similar aims were listed as the rationale for creating in 1956 the Polish Canadian Women's Federation. The federation is characterized by its vibrant activity in completing its everyday statutory tasks and its ability to act on a wider scale. Its project "Polish Spirit," mentioned earlier in this book, showed numerous Canadians of non-Polish origin the contribution of Polish Canadians to the development of Ontario and other provinces and Canada as a whole. The media release on the occasion of the exposition at Toronto Metro Hall in May 2011 stated:

> The Polish Spirit Exhibit documents survival, perseverance, creativity—the true "Polish spirit." It highlights the stories of those born in Canada and those who arrived from Poland after the First and Second World Wars or post-Solidarity. They have proven that it is possible to build a strong community and contribute to the well-being of others through creative and constructive use of human talent. Showcasing real stories, real lives and true records of personal achievement throughout Canadian history, the Exhibit shares Polish heritage with the community and shows Polish-Canadians are an integral part of the Canadian mosaic.

The federation closely cooperates with Polish-language schools in all provinces, understanding its mandate as the caretakers of Polish national traditions.

POLISH COMBATANTS ASSOCIATION OF CANADA

Since the end of World War II, Canada became a home to a large number of Polish veterans. Their organization is the Polish Combatants Association (Polish acronym SPK, for Stowarzyszenie Polskich

Kombatantów) established in 1946 as a Canadian chapter of an international organization of the same name. The SPK in turn is a member of the World Veteran Federation. Once very energetic and active, its level of activity decreases with the thinning ranks of Polish Canadian veterans.

ASSOCIATION OF POLISH ENGINEERS IN CANADA

The first group of Polish engineers, approximately 20 people, arrived in Halifax in March 1941. According to the decision made in London, on June 15, 1941, a meeting was organized in Ottawa, which in the chronicles of Stowarzyszenie Techników Polskich (STP)—Association of Polish Technicians—is regarded as the first general meeting of the association. The list of people present at the meeting included 29 names. A decision of fundamental importance was reached; the initiating members decided to form an Association of Polish Technicians in Canada independent of the parent organization of the same name, active since 1940 in England and other countries of the world, where Polish technicians and engineers found refuge during World War II.

The Canadian organization elected an independent board of directors and a review committee. In May 1942, at the second general meeting, the association already represented 112 members. Forty of them came from Great Britain, 58 from France, eight from Japan and six from Brazil.

This first group greatly contributed to the Canadian defence industry and their contribution was highly regarded by the Canadian authorities. The achievements of the Polish engineers and scientists were described with approval on June 23, 1946, in the "Proceedings of the Standing Committee on Immigration and Labour" of the Senate of Canada.

After 1945, STP was forced to alter its mandate. Because of the changed geopolitical situation in the world—with the expansion of the Soviet empire into Polish lands and into the territories of other East European countries—the association was no longer an organization of specialists who remained in Canada temporarily for the duration of World War II and who planned to return to their native country. Mainly through the efforts of the Toronto branch of the association, its members actively pursued a policy of convincing the Canadian authorities to allow Polish engineers and other specialists to come to Canada. As a result, approximately 270 Polish engineers found their new home in Canada in the following years.

STP members from the Ottawa branch actively participated in and contributed to the work of the Royal Commission on Bilingualism and Biculturalism, whose achievements were the foundation of Canada's multiculturalism. The Ottawa branch began the initiative of relief help to the Catholic University of Lublin (Katolicki Uniwersytet Lubelski—KUL). The Ottawa branch was also the main organizer of the nation-wide celebrations of the 500th birthday of Mikołaj Kopernik, which ended with the presentation of a spectroscope from the Canadian People for the University of Toruń Observatory.

The changes that occurred in Poland after 1989, with the return of sovereignty of the country, resulted again in drastic change in the association policy. A new Committee of Technological Collaboration with

Poland was formed in 1990—to organize lectures and collaborate with Polish universities and colleges, to offer assistance to the Polish representatives visiting Canada and to help with translation of publications. At present, the Association of Polish Engineers (renamed in 1996 as Stowarzyszenie Inżynierów Polskich—SIP) in Canada operates branches in Montréal, Ottawa, Toronto, Kitchener, Edmonton, Hamilton, Oshawa, Mississauga and Peterborough and has approximately 500 members. The association's primary objective is to find new forms of organizational life that meet the expectations of all members and to represent different age groups and different degrees of connections with Poland.

CANADA-POLAND CHAMBER OF COMMERCE OF TORONTO
This organization was created with the aim of promotion, development and expansion of business, trade and investment opportunities between Canada and Poland. It also strives to develop relations and networking opportunities with other ethnic business organizations in Canada. The chamber's work supplements the initiatives of both Canadian and the Polish government agencies.

POLISH SCOUTING ASSOCIATION IN CANADA
The Polish-language acronym of this association is ZHP (Związek Harcerstwa Polskiego), and it works to realize the same goals as the world scouting movement, with a particular focus on Polish national traditions. The association grew out of three groups of Polish scouts in Montréal, Ottawa and Toronto in the years from 1948 to 1951. Formerly, Polish scout troops functioned within the organizational framework of

the Canadian scouting movement. Today, the association directs the activities of several thousand members from Montréal to Edmonton, Calgary and Vancouver.

The relatively high level of education of Polish immigrants to Canada after World War II led to the establishment of two rather unusual immigrant organizations: the Polish Scientific Institute in Canada and the Canadian Polish Research Institute.

Polish Scientific Institute in Canada

The institute was established in 1943 thanks to the initiative of a renowned historian named Professor Oskar Halecki. He was at that time a lecturer in history at the University of Montréal and proposed that the Polish scientists living there should form a separate chapter of the institute, already in existence in the United States. The concept was reportedly an idea suggested to him by Wanda Stachiewicz, the organizer and for many years the director of the Polish Library, which is associated with the library collections of McGill University and today bears her name.

The members of the institute do not necessarily have Polish origin; it is enough to have an interest in Polish culture, history, art and science. That is why its list of members includes Professor Wilder Penfield of McGill University, Professor J.B. Colip of the Royal Society of Canada, Professor J. Rousseau of Association canadienne-française pour l'avancement des sciences, the McGill University professors W. Bovey, R.A. MacLennan and C. MacMillan, as well as other scientists interested and concerned by the state of Polish science. Polish members include Professor J. Pawlikowski, the dean of École Polytechnique de Montréal;

Professor B. Szczeniowski of Montréal University; and T. Poznański from Laval University, among others.

In 1976 the Montréal chapter of the Polish Scientific Institute in the United States evolved into a separate institution, the Polish Scientific Institute in Canada, which at present has three new chapters working in Ottawa, Toronto and Vancouver, and the process of establishing a chapter in Halifax is well underway. The main activity of the institute is organizing lectures and discussions, although occasionally the institute provides assistance to its members in publishing their scientific work.

CANADIAN POLISH RESEARCH INSTITUTE

The CPRI in Toronto is a non-profit organization that attracts people of Polish origin who are interested in research on the history, culture, language and social changes of the Polish ethnic minority in Canada. The chief task of the organization is to collect and preserve all documents concerning the life and work of Polish immigrants in Canada. The aim of the institute is to create an adequate source base for scientific research. The founder of the CPRI was Wiktor Turek. The first meeting organized upon the initiative of the Toronto Branch of the Canadian Polish Congress was held in Toronto on September 12, 1956. "There was a profound need, felt for a long time amidst Canadian Polonia," explained Dr. Turek, "for calling to life a research body that would be responsible for the study of problems connected with the development of a Polish ethnic group in Canada, which is one of the component groups of Canadian population and one of the contributing forces in the creation of a common Canadian culture."

The newly founded institute started its work by seeking and assembling documents and sources of information. Gradually, beginning with a small collection of brochures—mainly commemorative books of the various Polish organizations—the institute created a specialized and well-equipped workshop with a basic tool: a library. The institute's website states:

> Archives are the birth certificate of a nation, its collective memory made permanent in a material form. The Polish element within the Canadian cultural heritage reaches back to 1812, when Poles served in the regiments of de Meuron and de Watteville. Since that time, participation in the life of Canada of those arriving from Poland can be noted in every period of this country's history. Documentation for this is held in the CPRI archives. It allows researchers to reach the origins, which are fundamental for education, upbringing, and scientific and cultural development.

Initially, the institute planned to publish one book a year. The first five volumes published were written by Wiktor Turek, who had a reputation of being a workaholic. His ambition and goal in his work was to emphasize the contributions made by Poles to Canadian culture.

An important series of publications by the institute are six (so far) volumes of memoirs by Polish immigrants who came to Canada following World War II. The institute is presently collecting material for the next volume, dealing with the Solidarity wave of immigrants from Poland to Canada after 1981.

The manuscripts of the published volumes were prepared for publication by Benedykt Heydenkorn. They are doubtlessly excellent research material for further scientific studies. Overall, in the last 50 years, the institute published over 50 books, so the institute is fulfilling its mandate in spite of the rising costs of print publishing.

In 1978 the institute undertook the task of presenting its materials to the general public, not only to the Polish community. "Polish Perspectives" and "Polonica Canadiana" expositions were organized in the building of the Metropolitan Library in Toronto, where hundreds of daily visitors could view them.

Each exposition was complemented by a map showing the number of Poles in Canada, as well as the percentage of the entire population these numbers represented. Pictures documenting the life of Polish settlers in Alberta and in the Kaszuby region in Ontario—many from private collections and quite a few from before World War II—were of great interest because of their archival value.

THE CANADIAN POLISH HISTORICAL SOCIETY

Founded in 2005, the organization based in Edmonton is dedicated to the advancement of the knowledge and studies of Polish history, traditions and culture. Its main goal is to collect and archive important historical records of the achievements of people of Polish descent in Edmonton and throughout the province. It keeps the records of Canadian Polish immigrants and organizes and sponsors exhibitions, lectures and seminars.

POLISH MUSEUM SOCIETY "OGNIWO," WINNIPEG

According to the declaration found on its website, "The museum's mission is to develop an awareness and understanding of the Polish experience in Canada in current and future generations of Canadians, presenting our stories through exhibitions, presentations, workshops and special events. Its members share a vision of promoting of the Polish experience in Manitoba and Canada, the collection and preservation of artifacts reflecting both rural and urban lifestyles, and the exploration and exhibition of Polish history, traditions and folklore."

POLISH FOLK DANCING ORGANIZATIONS

Poles in Canada take great pride in their national culture and their achievements. For some unexplained reason, the true national culture is perceived as connected with folk dancing. Although not as characteristic as Irish or Scottish dancing, Polish folk dances are vibrant, captivating and spectacular when performed with gusto and skill. Almost all Polish Canadian communities tend to organize, sooner or later, a folk dance ensemble, teaching those dances to children of Polish immigrants. And they present them readily for the general Canadian public whenever invited. The ensembles exist all over Canada. The following are a few examples.

Polish Folk Dance Ensemble Pomorze in Halifax

Created in 1983, the ensemble had been "dormant" for several years. However, it has recently been reborn, and rehearsals are once again in progress. Since 2003, Pomorze has grown from a small group of enthusiasts to a well-organized company with a full repertoire.

The cast gave over 150 performances at occasions such as the Polish Dance Festival of the Americas in both Boston and Montréal; the Canadian Polish Dance Festival in Toronto; the Seventh and Eighth International Festival of Polish Folk Dance Ensembles in Rzeszów, Poland; the Canada Games Festivities in Cape Breton; the artistic program prepared for the visit of His Holiness Pope John-Paul II in Halifax as well as many other multicultural events and festivities.

Pomorze's performances in Poland earned them the Medal of Honour from among the 55 troupes from 11 countries that participated. The ensemble also produced two 30-minute television programs for Halifax Cablevision entitled *Zabawa–Poland Dances*.

Pomorze's costume collection is one of the best of its kind in Canada. The group can dazzle the audience with six complete colourful sets of eight men's and women's costumes for the dances in its repertoire. All the costumes are authentic folk production, usually made in their respective regions of Poland. The original music to which the dances are performed was scored for eight instruments and recorded by local musicians.

Tatry Polish Folklore Ensemble
"Founded in 1973 as a means of maintaining and preserving Polish culture in Montréal through the presentation of traditional dances, the Ensemble is made up of first, second and third-generation Canadians, all of Polish descent, who serve as ambassadors of Polish culture to the Polish Community and the general public," states this group's website.

The ensemble started with eight children, but now it comprises 60 amateur dancers, aged five to 30. The troupe performs extensively in Greater Montréal, participating at events organized for the Polish Community of Montréal, but it has shown its merit at various municipal multicultural festivals in Québec and Ontario, as well as in the United States and Poland. The ensemble does not disregard its location—its repertoire includes two Québec folk dances.

In Ontario, there are at least 12 Polish folk dance ensembles, some of which are in Brantford, Guelph, Hamilton, Kitchener, London, Mississauga, Oshawa and Toronto.

Hejnał Song and Dance Ensemble

Hejnał in Brantford has at present 65 members aging from three to 18 years of age. The group has presented its skill in folk dance to audiences in southern Ontario for almost 40 years. Some of its venues have included London, Kitchener, Woodstock, Cambridge, Delhi, Toronto at the CNE, a Blue Jays game, and CHIN picnic. It has also participated in the International Folklore Festival in Rzeszów, Poland.

Kujawiacy Polish Song and Dance Ensemble

Formed in May 1992 in Kitchener, the group is working hard on developing authentic and artistic Polish cultural entertainment. In April 2001, Kujawiacy invited to Kitchener a Polish folk dance group from Belarus named Karolinka. The two ensembles gave a concert from which Kujawiacy donated a sum of $1500 to Karolinka to cover their travel expenses from Belarus to Canada. At the end of April, Kujawiacy travelled to Ottawa to host a Folklorama performance for spectators in Canada's capital city. In June 2003, the City of Belleville invited Kujawiacy to attend its multicultural event to entertain a wide audience of onlookers. In 2004, the annual Children's Festival was held in MarryHill, with special guests Krakusy from Calgary.

Swarni

This group out of Mississauga belongs to the younger generation of Polish folk dance ensembles in Canada, as it was created in 2001. A substantial number of its members are second-generation Polish Canadians. The group's main region of interest in Poland is the mountainous south of the country, with the area's world-famous Góralski dances. Swarni organized a highland music band that teaches children to play folk music of the region.

The Swarni website states:

> The group entertains their audiences with breathtaking programs of the cultural dances and songs from the highlander region, and shows filled with highlander traditions, such as the famous making of "oscypki," a type of cheese. All program ideas are derived from tales of the past, coming from the people that were once shepherds in the highlands.

Lechowia

Established in Toronto in 1977 as an amateur dance organization, Lechowia was named after Lech, a Polish national hero who, according to the legend, founded the Polish nation. Today, the company has over 200 dancers, singers and musicians from all age groups. Lechowia's rich collection of program elements presents several different choreographic arrangements from all over Poland. Its audience can be acquainted with the slow, elegant dances such as the Mazur and the Polonaise popularized by Frederic Chopin; the dynamic Polka; the spectacular Krakowiak; the fast-paced Oberek; and the Góralski highland dance that never fails to move the audience. The dance program is complemented by charming vocals based on the music of the Silesia region.

The management of the ensemble stresses the theory that the expression of Polish folk culture is something more than traditional folk dancing. The dynamic staging of the dances and the cast's use of comedy and theatrics, supplemented by ballads, transcends the limited boundaries of folk dance performances and reaches into the region of non-ethnic popular entertainment. The method of organizing their performance brought success to the ensemble and is appreciated by their audience. Over the years, Lechowia has repeatedly been awarded important recognition, including honours for Best Entertainment, Best Musical Theatre, Choreography, and for Staging and Costumes for their performance at the Metro International Caravan Festival's Kraków Pavilion in Toronto.

Although organized to propagate Polish culture, Lechowia stresses that its home is Canada, and the group displays the maple leaf during its international travels. The group has toured the United States, performing from Boston to San Francisco, and has appeared in Australia (Canada Pavilion at Expo '88 in Brisbane), France and Spain (1994), Taiwan (Canadian representation at World Folklore Festival, 1999) and Mexico (2000). The group also participated in the

International Polish Folk Festivals in Rzeszów in 1980, 1983 and 1989; in Iwonicz in 1997 and in Kielce in 2000.

Sokół Polish Folk Ensemble

The senior member of this group of Polish dance ensembles, Sokół was established in 1915. Its history is closely connected with the history of the Polish Gymnastic Association Sokół, established by Polish immigrants in Winnipeg in 1906. There are no records that definitely state when the Sokół choir was first formed, but the choir performed at the opening of the Sokół Association in the fall of 1914. Directed by Kazimierz Sielski, the first recorded performance in front of the Canadian public took place at Winnipeg's Walker Theatre.

In 1937, American filmmakers asked the ensemble to present the Polonaise and other songs and dances to be recorded on film at the Royal Alexandra Ballroom. In 1952, the ensemble was filmed and photographed by Yousuf Karsh, the unquestionable master of portrait photography of the 20th century. Led by Richard Seaborn, the Sokół choir won the Lord Tweedsmuir Trophy at the Manitoba Music Festival in 1964 and sang in a series of concerts with the Winnipeg Symphony Orchestra.

The Sokół choir is proud of its numerous radio performances and of having been presented in the CBC series *Au Coin du Terre* in 1975 and the CTV series *In Harmony* in 1983. For their 70th anniversary, the choir recorded two albums, one of Polish folk and popular songs, the other of Christmas carols. The group does not limit its program to folk repertoire;

it has an extensive selection of liturgical, serious and classical music. Sixty singers, dancers and musicians work hard to acquaint their audiences with Polish culture as expressed in song and dance, but it has also ventured into the territory of opera and operettas.

Polonia Polish Folk Dance Ensemble

"The Polonia Polish Folk Dance Ensemble (PPFDE) has been a part of the cultural life of Regina since the 1930s," states the organization's website. "As Polish immigrants settled in Regina, they congregated around St. Anthony's Roman Catholic Church, the 'Polish Church.' At first the dance group was simply a social club for husbands and wives who had recently immigrated to Canada. However, dancing soon became an important way to preserve the Polish culture in Regina and area."

There are presently 65 members of the ensemble, ranging in age from four to 50 years. They perform at various Polish shows and festivities, including artistic programs organized for Canada Day. Polonia has taken part in such events as the Regina Oktoberfest (1978), Prairie Lily Folk Ballet (1980) and Dickinson Ethnic Festival in North Dakota (1986, 1987). They were at the Winnipeg Folklorama many times, and they participated in a fundraiser for the historic Our Lady of Assumption Co-Cathedral in Gravelbourg.

In 2001, Polonia was especially honoured to perform for His Royal Highness Prince Charles during his visit to Regina City Hall. In early October 2004, Polonia visited Edmonton to help celebrate the city's 100-year anniversary.

Polanie Polish Song and Dance Association

Founded in 1977 in Calgary, the aim of the group is to present the richness of Polish folklore in a stylized artistic adaptation. Since its outset, the ensemble has developed and established a unique style that has become a recognized landmark both in Canada and abroad.

Polanie has represented Calgary and Canada at performances and festivals in Canada, the United States and Poland. The ensemble is a regular highlight at multicultural festivals in Calgary and also takes part in the celebrations of Canada Day, Heritage Day and the Winter Festival. The group has presented its program at Festival of Nations at the Spruce Meadows Masters and had the honour of performing at the opening ceremonies of the 1988 Calgary Winter Olympics and at the 1997 World Police and Fire Games in Calgary. High artistic standard has also been demonstrated at the Festival of Folk Dance in Boston (1987), San Francisco (1995), Los Angeles (1995, 1997), Toronto (2002), Regina (2007) and Kimberley (2007).

Polonez Polish Folk Arts Ensemble

The group from Edmonton was created in 1982 to uphold Polish culture, customs and folklore and to be part of the great Canadian mosaic. Today, Polonez boasts a wide repertoire of authentic folklore from the central and southern regions of Poland. Accompanying the repertoire are over 300 authentic costumes. Polonez has had the honour of staging over 1000 performances for a wide variety of audiences in Edmonton, across Alberta and Canada, and in Poland. Polonez annually gives 25 to 30 volunteer performances for a variety of organizations, including hospitals and schools in the Edmonton area.

A Polonez performance is a whirlwind tour through hundreds of years of Polish folk culture. From the stately court dances of the nobility to the lively dances of the Polish countryside, Polonez strives to bring the vibrancy of Polish folk culture to audiences everywhere.

Oberek Polish Canadian Children's Dance Society

Oberek was named after a Polish dance, and the group was formed in 1986 by members of the Polish community in Edmonton in order to cultivate Polish culture and heritage. It attracted children from five to 16 years of age. The directors of the ensemble stress the experience of the grace and poise of Polish folklore for the participants. The society provides children an opportunity to play in an artistic environment, while at the same time acquiring first-hand knowledge of Polish heritage. The dancers get the opportunity to travel, visit other cities in Canada and abroad, make new friends and share unforgettable memories of performing in front of different audiences.

Polonez Polish Canadian Dance Society

This ensemble from Vancouver was founded in 1989. It started mainly as a place of interest for older enthusiasts of Polish folk song and dance. Later, after the first performance in 1990, the group began to attract younger devotees. Presently, Polonez consists of over 100 active members and, as they say, has become an integral part of Vancouver's artistic and cultural stage as well as being the city's Polish cultural ambassador.

Song and dance would seem to be the main pastime of Polish Canadians, judging by the number and achievements of the ensembles. This is, however, a simplification: various Polish-founded clubs and organizations exist all over the country, and most of them, while Polish in origin, welcome all Canadians.

WHITE SAILS: POLISH CANADIAN YACHT CLUB

As stated on this GTA sailing club's website, "Our club is a not-for-profit organization that was created to serve mostly sailors and boaters of Polish origin, but everybody is welcome. We operate on Lake Ontario and Georgian Bay." In March 2011, the former commodore of the club, Michał Bogusławski, set out on a solo voyage around the world under Canadian and Polish flags. The voyage may take a few years.

ZAWISZA CZARNY: POLISH CANADIAN YACHT CLUB

Yacht Club Zawisza Czarny (YCZC), was created in 1996 in Hamilton as an association of Polish Canadian sailors but has since developed into a Canadian institution, and its annual May match-racing regatta always attracts all manner of sailors, some of whom have no connection to Poland. Although the club is relatively small, its members successfully compete in world championships in class J-24 (2006 in Australia, 2009 in the USA). The club is also the co-organizer of the Sea Shanties Festival that has been part of the GTA cultural calendar since 2006.

POLISH CANADIAN WINDSURFING CLUB OF BC

This club brings together sailors and windsurfers of various experience and abilities, and its website stresses that all are welcome to join and have fun together. The emphasis of the club members is on relaxation, not on sport achievements. That is why in winter, the interests of the members change, and the Polish Canadian Windsurfing Club of BC becomes the Polish Canadian Skiing/Snowboarding Club of BC.

THE NOVA SCOTIA SOCIETY OF POLISH ARTISTS

This society in Halifax was established in 2007. Its members include Canadian artists of Polish origin living and working in Nova Scotia. The Polish Canadian population of the province is not large, with numbers probably no more than 4000 people. The society, however, demonstrates exceptional energy in its endeavours and creativity in planning events for the public. Within only three years of its activity, the club has presented about a dozen shows and expositions, including involvement in the annual Nocturne nighttime festival at Pier 21.

LA CORPORATION QUÉBEC POLOGNE POUR LES ARTS

Since 1998, this organization out of Montréal tirelessly works toward organizing cultural events promoting the cultural achievements of Poland in Québec. Its aim is to construct and expand the cultural cooperation between the two societies of Poland and Québec. Films, art expositions, theatrical spectacles, literary readings, debates and publications are just some of the activities that connect the two areas. The organization closely cooperates with such institutions of Québec culture as Cinematheque québecoise, Prospero Theatre, Place des Arts, Galeria Espace Creation, and the Université du Québec à Montréal.

McGill Polish Students Association
Polish Student Association at York University
Polish Students Club, University of Calgary
Polish Students Society at UBC
Polish Students Union at UWO

Students of Polish origin tend to form their associations at universities all over Canada. They bring some of that warm Polish culture (and those delicious perogies) to their community, as well as tirelessly working to organize diverse activities to ensure maximum participation of their members.

Polish Canadian Coin and Stamp Club "Troyak"

"Troyak" is an officially registered member of the Ontario Numismatic Association as well as a member at the Greater Toronto Area Philatelic Alliance. The club is a non-profit organization that, since 2004, has been providing assistance in dealing with issues concerning coins and stamps. The club welcomes all people interested in the education and study in numismatics and philately.

Polonia Sport Club

Founded before World War II, this club in Windsor was revived in 1982 after a period of inactivity. It provides facilities primarily for soccer (eight teams at various age levels) but also for enthusiasts of volleyball, gymnastics, tennis, table tennis and judo.

Olympium Rhythmic Gymnastics Club

ORGC was started in 1986 by two enthusiasts of the sport, Danuta Śmiechowska and Małgorzata Wichrowska, immigrants from Poland. The club, based in Etobicoke, quickly achieved a high standard of training and became popular with parents who wanted their daughters to benefit through participation in this elegant sport. Rhythmic gymnastics combines physical exercise and control of movement with a musical background and elegance of posture. The club offers both recreational and competitive programs, suitable for all girls and young women regardless of their gymnastic aptitude and talent.

MISSISSAUGA FENCING CLUB

This club was founded by Marian Zakrzewski, one of the most successful Polish fencers, who coached the Polish Olympic sabre team for the Montréal Olympics in 1976 and the Canadian sabre team for the Seoul Olympics in 1988. The club offers a wide range of programs from pre-fencing classes for young children (age 3–6), introduction to fencing classes for youth, teenagers and adults to advanced competitive training. MFC members participate in league competitions on a regular basis and have had success. Matthew McLeod won a silver medal at the 2008 Junior World Cup in Montréal, and, in 2009, gold, silver and bronze at the Arnold Fencing Classic competition in Columbus, Ohio. Kamil Karbonowski took a bronze at the event in 2006, and a bronze medal at the 2009 national championships of Canada.

GDAŃSK ASSOCIATION

This organization invites all people originally from the major Polish port city of Gdańsk. The club is informal and it holds monthly meetings and an annual ball. However, it does try to present basic information about its beloved city to anyone wishing to listen.

We Can Do It Together

There are over 200 organizations formed by Polish Canadians. Some of those organizations are almost 100 years old and have impressive achievements on their books, others burst with spontaneous energy from time to time or remained dormant at other times, awaiting another pretext to renewed activity. They are run almost exclusively by volunteers devoting their time and energy to achieving common goals. In almost all cases the associations are an expression of sentiment to Poland and of sentiment for the national culture and traditions that should be preserved and transmitted to younger generations of Polish Canadians. Such is their main declared aim, stressed in their charters or as expressed on their websites.

Some cynically-minded advocates of ethnic integration may be of an opinion that the goals and achievements of these organizations are marginal and unimportant. The membership in these organizations comprises less than 10 percent of the total of almost one million Canadians who can trace their roots to Poland. The vast majority of Polish Canadians remaining outside these organizations participate in activities as spectators or join purely Canadian clubs and unions, disregarding linguistic and ethnic unity. It has been said many times in various discussions and publications in the Polish community that the organizations have outlived their usefulness and their demise is a matter of time. The pronouncements were made in the 1950s, after the wave of veterans settled in their new land, and in the 1980s, when the thousands of "new" Polish Canadians arrived and decreed the organizations outdated and moribund.

The organizations, however, still play an important role today. They still occasionally are forced to defend Polish people in Canada against injustice or discrimination, they help Polish immigrants to settle in the new land with as few problems as possible, and, first and foremost, they work toward the creation of a positive image of the Polish in Canada. They try to ease the process of cultural acclimatization in the interest of both the immigrants and the host society.

JOHN PAUL II POLISH CULTURAL CENTRE

This centre in Mississauga has been in existence since 1994. It is possibly the most active, dynamic and effective centre of everything Polish in Canada. The centre works to preserve and foster the heritage of Canadians of Polish descent as well as to serve the needs of the greater community. Various cultural, educational and recreational programs are offered as well as a range of facilities to hold business, art, sport and social events. Many of the activities are connected to the Polish heritage. Some, however, are not—they are Canadian in character.

At the beginning of the Polish timeline in the history of Canada, there were no Polish organizations mainly because of minimal numbers of Polish immigrants and the geographical factors of Polish settlement in Canada—from the Rockies through Winnipeg all the way to Toronto and northern Ontario. The onset of the 20th century brought into existence some self-help organizations founded to assist its members in building their new life in Canada and to defend them against discrimination. Whatever organizational life there was, it became concentrated around the church in their parish.

World War II changed everything—including the area of interest of the Polish immigration. Manitoba and the Prairies were replaced by Montréal, Ottawa and Toronto as new places to settle. Polish organizations had excellent connections and extended intensive cooperation with similar associations outside Canada, basing it on the wartime experience of their members. They profited from strong ties binding comrades in arms. It was the "golden age" of Polish organizations in Canada, but the energy slowly faded to almost nothing with the aging of its membership.

The final phase began with 1981 and the anti-Solidarity crackdown of the Communist authorities in Poland. Many experienced activists found their way to Canada and continued their interest in organizational life of the community. Polish organizations in Canada were revived, changed or replaced by new forms of activity. To an extent, this legacy is still here with us, but from year to year these types of organizations play a lesser role in the life of the community.

Polish Canadians, taking advantage of the politics of multiculturalism, thanks to changes in social attitudes, now without fear of discrimination and prejudice, take an increasingly more active part in the life of Canada. The Polish Canadian organizations have played their role and achieved their ends. Now the time has come for Polish Canadians to show themselves as expert players on the wide Canadian arena.

APPENDIX II

IT PAYS TO BE CANADIAN

At the beginning of this book I related a story of Nils von Schoultz, who successfully entered Canadian history pretending to be Polish. Complementing this story are vastly popular books in Poland, Russia and a few other countries, authored by Stanisław Supłatowicz under the pen-name of Sat-Okh, or "Long Feather." The phenomenon of Grey Owl—an Englishman who pretended to be Native—has its Polish equivalent, if somewhat less well known.

According to his autobiographical information, Sat-Okh was the son of a Polish young woman and a Canadian Shawnee chief. He pretended to have been born in the wilderness of the Canadian North sometime in April 1920. In 1937 he reportedly returned to the land of his mother, took part in the Polish underground resistance movement during World War II and was decorated for his bravery and achievements. After the war Supłatowicz was persecuted by the Communist authorities, to finally serve in the Polish merchant marine. He wrote youth fiction books and popularized the story of Native people in Poland.

Sat-Okh insisted that his mother, Stanisława Supłatowicz, came from a noble family persecuted by tsarist Russia for political reasons. Her family was exiled to Siberia in 1905, and 12 years later, the young Polish woman managed to escape in the company of other Polish exiles and made her way east, to finally reach the Bering Strait. Carried over the water by friendly Chukchi Natives of eastern Siberia, she ended up on the American continent, in Alaska. From there, for unexplained reasons, she reportedly continued walking east into Canada and almost died of hunger and exhaustion, when she was found and saved from death by hunters from a local Shawnee tribe.

Shawnee chief Leoo-Karko-Ono-Ma, a descendant of a historical Shawnee leader Tecumseh, fell in love with the blonde woman of exotic beauty, married her and they had three children. Sat-Okh was the youngest child. Although his physical appearance showed traces of his mixed Polish-Shawnee blood, Sat-Okh was raised Shawnee and enjoyed all the training the Shawnees provided for their youth. It was, so he said, to come in useful in absolutely unexpected circumstances.

In 1937 Sat-Okh accompanied his mother on a visit to her native Poland. There, he fell in love with his new homeland and decided to stay. Documents from that

Stanisław Supłatowicz, or Sat-Okh (on the left and inset), a friend of Native Canadians

period confirm the existence of Stanisław Supłatowicz (his new first name was a masculine form of his mother's first name) but do not mention anything about his Native father. Reportedly, the omission was done to protect him from racist persecution.

The decision to stay in Poland proved fateful. Two years later, Nazi Germany invaded Poland, and Supłatowicz joined the underground resistance army. He was arrested in 1940, tortured and finally sent with a death warrant to the infamous Auschwitz concentration camp. According to his autobiographical notes and pronouncements, while in transport to Auschwitz, he used the skills he had acquired in the Canadian wilderness, as well as his Native bravery and physical fitness, to escape from the transport, helping other prisoners to escape at the same time. Sat-Okh disappeared into the Polish forests, later on joined a unit of the Home Army and spent the rest of the war fighting the Nazi occupation forces in the Świętokrzyskie Mountains in central Poland. He was honoured for his exploits with high military decorations, awarded to him during and after the war.

His post-war biography was devoid of further excitement. He completed his education and for a few years worked as a mechanic on Polish merchant ships. Finally, he decided to try his hand at storytelling, and after 1958 he authored several novels directed at young readers, telling first the story of his Native Canadian origins, and later on popularizing Canadian First Nation mythology, folk literature and customs. His books were translated into Russian, German, French, Japanese, Czech, Bulgarian, Ukrainian, Lithuanian, Estonian, Mongolian and even Hebrew languages.

In the 1970s, Supłatowicz made numerous TV appearances, recounting the story of his origin and sharing information about the Canadian North and its people. It has been repeatedly stressed that his activities brought an Eastern European audience closer to the history and culture of Native Canadians. He is credited with being one of the initiators of an informal organization in Poland called Polish Movement of Friends of the Indians. The movement led to establishing a unique museum. If you ever find yourself in a small village of Wymysłów in northern Poland, it may be of interest to visit the local Museum of North American Indians.

Supłatowicz died in Gdańsk in 2003. His memory is still cherished by Polish people fascinated with the history and culture of Canadian First Nations. The museum near Gdańsk is devoted to his memory and the story of his Native origins.

The story of Sat-Okh is charming, if not true. There were Polish exiles in Siberia, and some of them escaped (rarely successfully). The romance and marriage of a Polish young woman and a Shawnee chief is possible. What makes the story suspect are the geographical details. Sat-Okh and his father's tribe were supposed to have lived somewhere on the banks of the Mackenzie River. But according to historians, no Shawnees ever moved that far away from their original hunting grounds in the Ohio valley. There were some Shawnees living in the western United States, and there is a second Mackenzie River (much smaller and shorter than the one flowing from Great Slave Lake) in Oregon. However, if Supłatowicz was in fact born in this area, his story, contrary to his declarations, has nothing to do with Canada.

Poland is exotic to Canadians. And Canada—despite that about one million of its inhabitants have some connection to Poland—is still considered an exotic and unknown land to millions of Poles. Maybe it is time to do something about it—maybe it's time to devote more energy to presenting Canada, its history and its achievements to the Polish people? And, conversely, presenting the achievements of Polish people to Canadians? This book is an attempt at the latter.

Notes on Sources

Borowczyk-Forester, Jan. *In Search of Freedom.* Toronto: Canadian Polish Research Institute, 2000.

Bothwell, Robert, Ian Drummond, and John English. *Canada Since 1945.* Toronto: University of Toronto Press. 1989.

Creighton, Donald G. *The Young Politician.* Toronto: University of Toronto Press, 1998.

Czas-Związkowiec (The Alliancer), Toronto: Polish Alliance in Canada, October 1, 2005.

Fontana, James. *The Mad Bomber of Parliament Hill.* Ottawa: Borealis Press, 2005.

Grabowski, Stanisław. "André Loup: Le premier colon polonais en Nouvelle-France," Actes du Colloque de l'Institut polonais des Arts et des Sciences au Canada, Ottawa, 1995.

Henoch, W.E.S. *One Man Many Lives.* Toronto: Canadian Polish Research Institute. n.d.

Heydenkorn, Benedykt. *A Community in Transition.* Toronto: Canadian Polish Research Institute, 1985.

Heydenkorn, Benedykt (ed.). *Pamiętniki imigrantów polskich w Kanadzie, Tom II* (Memoirs of Polish Immigrants to Canada, Vol. II), Toronto: Polish Alliance Press, 1977.

Kotz, Tadeusz. *Błękitne niebo i prawdziwe kule* (Blue Sky and Real Bullets). Toronto: 1307815 Ontario Limited, 2005.

Kujawa, Arkadiusz. *Polacy w Kanadzie* (Poles in Canada). Warszawa: ASPRA-JR, 2008.

Kusiba, Marek. *A Day in the Life: Janusz Zurakowski: From Avro Arrow to Arrow Drive.* Toronto: Adres Press, 2003.

Matejko, Joanna (ed.). *Reminiscences and Biographies.* Toronto: Polish Alliance Ltd., 1979.

Moir, John S., and D.M.L. Farr. *The Canadian Experience*. Toronto: McGraw-Hill Ryerson, 1969.

Reczyńska, Anna. *Polonia kanadyjska* (Polish Canadians), unpublished manuscript.

Renkiewicz, Frank. *The Polish Presence in Canada and America*. Toronto: Multicultural History Society of Ontario, 1982.

Stolarczyk, Stanisław. *Gdzie stopy nasze* (Where Our Footprints Are). Białystok: Arax, 1991.

Świderski, A.A. *Contribution of Polish Engineers and Architects to Canadian Life*. unpublished manuscript.

Turek, Victor. *Poles in Manitoba*. Toronto: Polish Research Institute in Canada, 1967.

Ziółkowska, Aleksandra. *Dreams and Reality*. Toronto: Adam Mickiewicz Foundation, 1984.

Ziółkowska-Boehm, Aleksandra. *The Roots Are Polish* (Translation of Korzenie są polskie, BGW, Warszawa), 2nd ed. Toronto: Canadian Polish Research Institute, 1992.

Web Sources

webdocs.cs.ualberta.ca/~smillie/ComputerAndMe/Part11.html

www.7news.pl/detail/53602

www.angelfire.com/ab/szwarctree/olek.html

www.biographi.ca

www.cahf.ca/members/Z_members.php

www.canadianpolishinstitute.org/home/welcome.html

www.digitaljournal.com/article/277263

www.en.wikipedia.org/wiki/Janusz_%C5%BBurakowski

www.evastachniak.com/www.evastachniak.com/
Eva_Stachniak.html/

www.federacjapolek.ca

www.indianie.eco.pl/litera/sat-okh1.html

www.janinafialkowska.com/biography.aspx

www.k-k.pl/dokumenty/bracia-kulawi.html

www.kpk.org/index.php?option=com_content&view
=article&id=122&Itemid=138

www.kujawiacy.com

www.members.shaw.ca/polonez/index.htm

www.muzeumhw.pl/1/111/424/Historie-rodzinne-
Leonard-Wiktor-Ramczykowski

www.oberek.ca

www.ontario.coop/edirectory/st_stanislausst_
casimirs_polish_parishes_credit_union_branch_2

www.polanie.ca

www.polcu.com/default.asp

www.polishculture.ca/en/profile/24

www.polisheng.ca/history.html

www.polishmuseum.com

www.poloniaregina.com

www.pomorzedance.com

www.quebec-pologne.ca/

www.rsc.ca/documents/BlachutTeodor19152004.pdf

www.sokolensemble.ca/history.htm

www.torontosinfonietta.com/history/

www12.statcan.ca/census-recensement/2006/dp-pd/
hlt/97-562/pages/page.cfm?Lang=E&Geo=PR&Co
de=01&Data=Count&Table=2&StartRec=1&Sort
=3&Display=All&CSDFilter=5000

Jacek Kozak

Jacek Kozak is a self-professed book-aholic who loves to travel. He graduated with a master's degree in English from the University of Warsaw, and he also obtained a master's degree in history from the University of Toronto in 1998. For 35 years, Jacek was a journalist for a variety of national and international media in Poland, Canada and the U.S. Currently he works on popularizing the achievements of Polish Canadians in Canada.